VIOLA BOOK 1

ESSENTIAL ELEMENTS for Strings

COMPREHENSIVE STRING METHOD

MICHAEL ALLEN • ROBERT GILLESPIE • PAMELA TELLEJOHN HAYES
ARRANGEMENTS BY JOHN HIGGINS

CONGRATULATIONS! You have made one of the most rewarding decisions in your life by joining the orchestra. The key to succeeding with *Essential Elements for Strings* is your commitment to daily practice. Each time you learn a new note, count a new rhythm, or play a melody with a friend, you become a more accomplished musician. As you continue to develop your skills, you will become increasingly aware of an abundance of opportunities that are available in the future. Musicians can teach, perform, conduct, or compose. No matter what profession you choose there are always opportunities available to you. You can play in community, civic, or church orchestras, attend concerts, and become a supporter of the arts. Whether you choose music as a vocation or avocation, we hope it will become an important part of your life. We are thrilled to welcome you to our orchestra family and wish you the very best for a lifetime of musical success.

HISTORY OF THE VIOLA

The string family includes the violin, viola, violoncello, and the double bass. The early ancestors of the string family were the Arabian rebab and rebec, popular during the 14th–16th centuries. The viola is the oldest of the modern string instruments, and the word "viola" was used to describe many different string instruments until the 18th century. Today's violas look like violins, though they are larger and longer.

The sound of the viola includes notes lower than the violin and has a particular mellow quality that is darker and richer. The viola is often referred to as the alto voice of the orchestra. Antonio Stradivari, and the Guarneri and Guadagnini families were famous instrument makers from the 17th and 18th centuries, and their violas are still in use today.

Many important composers have been violists, including Wolfgang Amadeus Mozart and Paul Hindemith. Other composers known for their viola compositions include Hector Berlioz, Ernest Bloch, and Béla Bartók. Famous viola performers include Walter Trampler, Lionel Tertis, Donald McGinnis, William Primrose, Nobuko Imai, and Kim Kashkashian.

To create an account, visit:
www.essentialelementsinteractive.com

Student Activation Code
E1VA-4592-0301-8150

ISBN 979-835012075-2

THE VIOLA

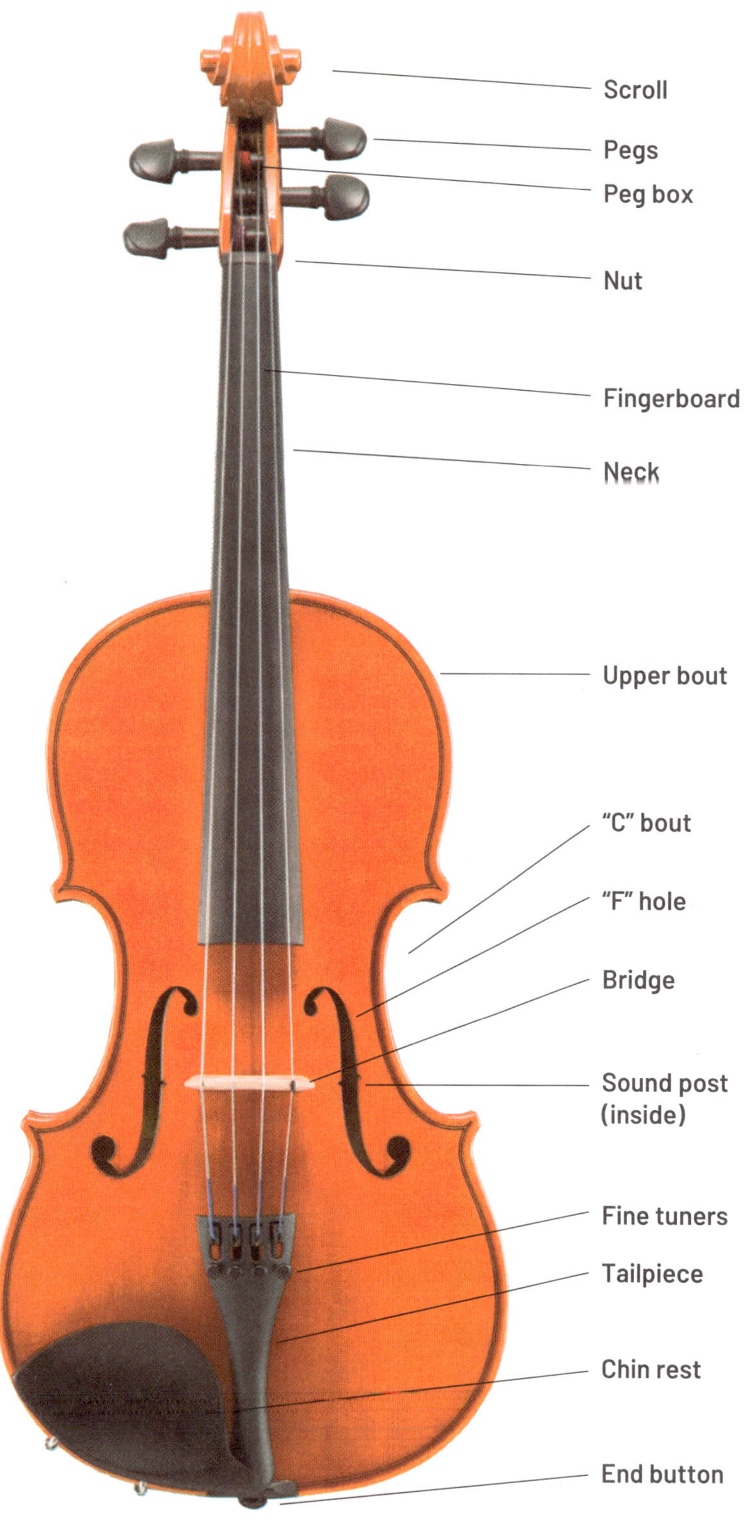

Take Special Care

String instruments are delicate. Follow your teacher's guidelines in caring for your instrument, and it will last forever.

- Follow your teacher's instructions when removing the instrument from the case.
- Protect your instrument from heat, cold, and quick changes in temperature.
- Always wipe off the instrument with a soft dry cloth. Be sure to remove all fingerprints and rosin.
- Place a cloth over the top of the viola before closing the case.

Accessories

- Rosin
- Shoulder rest
- Soft cloth
- Extra set of strings

Instruments and photos courtesy of Eastman Music Company.

THE BOW

- Never touch the bow hair.
- Keep the bow in your case until directed by your teacher.

Holding Your Instrument

The best way to learn to play your instrument is to practice one skill at a time. Repeat each step until you are comfortable demonstrating it for your teacher and classmates.

Many viola players begin by playing their instrument in guitar position. As you learn the basics, your teacher will help you change to shoulder position.

Guitar Position

Step 1 Place the instrument case flat on the floor with the handle facing you. Open the case and lift the instrument up by the neck. Identify all parts of the viola.

Step 2 Cradle the viola under your right arm. Raise the scroll to shoulder height. Be sure the back of the viola is flat against your stomach.

Step 3 Identify the letter names of each string: C (lowest pitch), G, D, A.

Step 4 Raise your right thumb over the strings while continuing to hold the instrument. Pluck the strings as directed by your teacher. Plucking the strings is called *pizzicato*, and is abbreviated *pizz.*

Shoulder Position

Step 1 *(Standing)* – Stand with feet about a shoulder's width apart. *(Sitting)* – Sit on the front part of the chair.

Step 2 Turn your left foot to the 10 o'clock position. Slide your right foot back. Adjust your position to place more weight on your left foot.

Step 3 Hold your instrument at eye level, parallel to the floor. Curve your left hand around the upper bout. Find the end button with your right hand.

Step 4 Bring the instrument down to your shoulder. The end button should be near the middle of your neck. Turn your head slightly to the left, and place your jaw on the chin rest. Be sure the scroll does not point toward the floor.

Guitar Position

Shoulder Position

The student shown is a member of the Milwaukee Youth Symphony Orchestra.

See inside front cover for information on accessing instructional videos.

SHAPING THE LEFT HAND

D STRING NOTES

Step 1 Shape your left hand as shown. Be certain your palm faces you.

0 = Open string
1 = 1st finger
2 = 2nd finger
3 = 3rd finger
4 = 4th finger

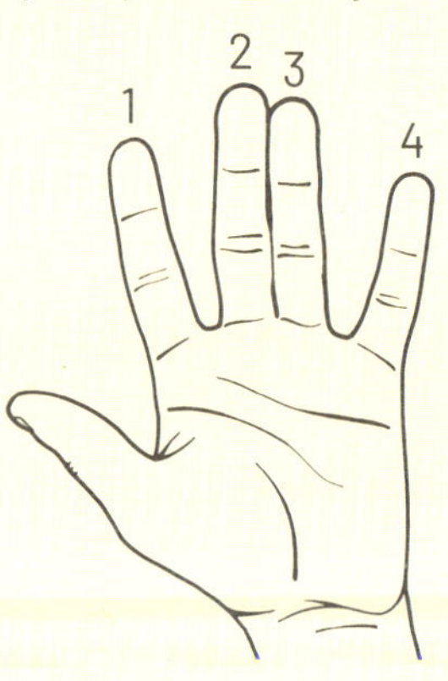

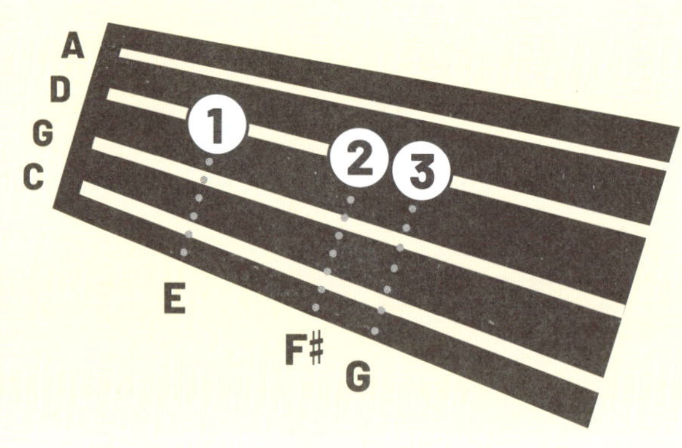

Step 2 Bring your hand to the fingerboard. Place your fingers on the D string, keeping your hand shaped as shown below. Be sure your 1st finger forms a square with the fingerboard, and your wrist is relaxed and straight.

G is played with 3 fingers on the D string.

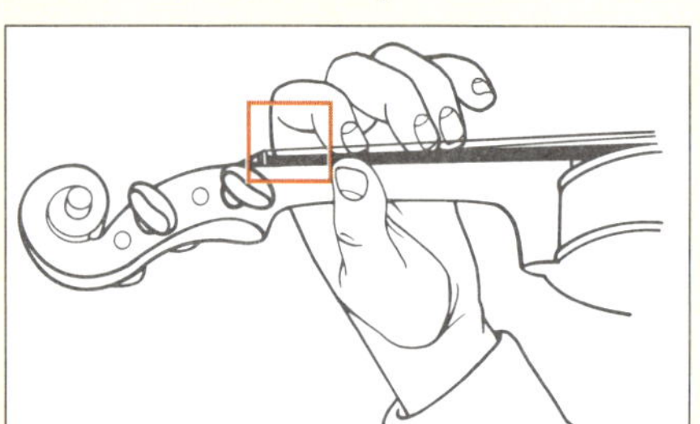

F♯ is played with 2 fingers on the D string.

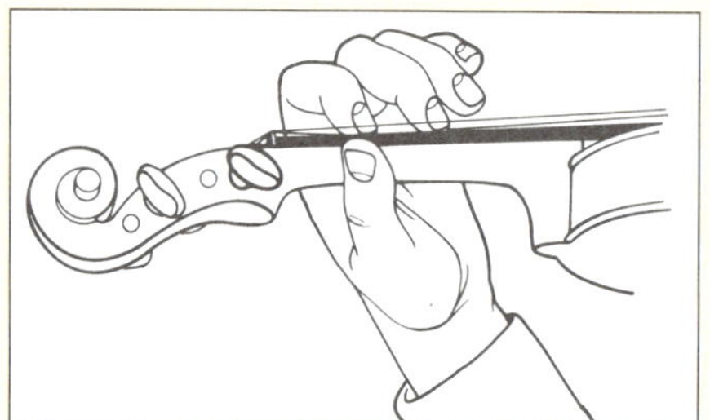

E is played with 1 finger on the D string.

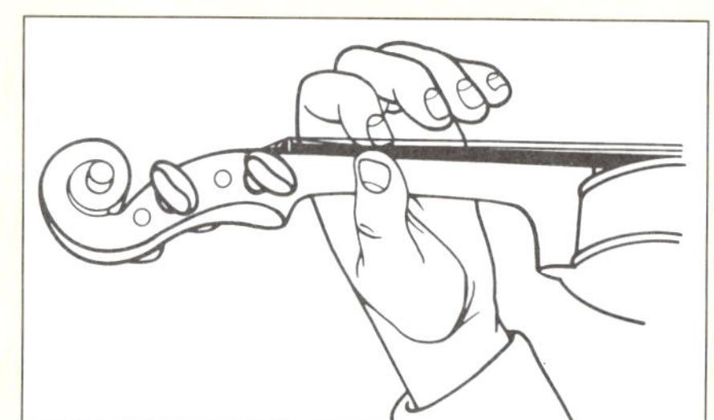

Listening Skills Play what your teacher plays. Listen carefully.

10. LET'S READ "G" *Start memorizing the note names.*

THEORY

Sharp ♯

A **sharp** sign raises the sound of notes and remains in effect for the entire measure. Notes without sharps are called **natural** notes.

11. LET'S READ "F♯" (F-sharp)

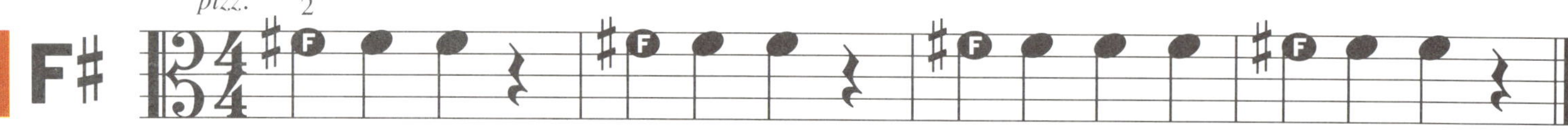

▲ *Play all F♯'s. Sharps apply to the entire measure.*

12. LIFT OFF

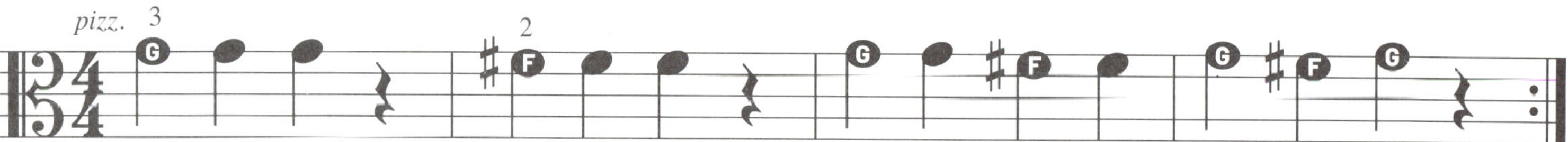

✔ Is your left hand shaped as shown in the diagrams above?

Holding Your Instrument

The best way to learn to play your instrument is to practice one skill at a time. Repeat each step until you are comfortable demonstrating it for your teacher and classmates.

Many viola players begin by playing their instrument in guitar position. As you learn the basics, your teacher will help you change to shoulder position.

Guitar Position

Step 1 Place the instrument case flat on the floor with the handle facing you. Open the case and lift the instrument up by the neck. Identify all parts of the viola.

Step 2 Cradle the viola under your right arm. Raise the scroll to shoulder height. Be sure the back of the viola is flat against your stomach.

Step 3 Identify the letter names of each string: C (lowest pitch), G, D, A.

Step 4 Raise your right thumb over the strings while continuing to hold the instrument. Pluck the strings as directed by your teacher. Plucking the strings is called *pizzicato*, and is abbreviated *pizz.*

Shoulder Position

Step 1 *(Standing)* – Stand with feet about a shoulder's width apart. *(Sitting)* – Sit on the front part of the chair.

Step 2 Turn your left foot to the 10 o'clock position. Slide your right foot back. Adjust your position to place more weight on your left foot.

Step 3 Hold your instrument at eye level, parallel to the floor. Curve your left hand around the upper bout. Find the end button with your right hand.

Step 4 Bring the instrument down to your shoulder. The end button should be near the middle of your neck. Turn your head slightly to the left, and place your jaw on the chin rest. Be sure the scroll does not point toward the floor.

Guitar Position

Shoulder Position

The student shown is a member of the Milwaukee Youth Symphony Orchestra.

See inside front cover for information on accessing instructional videos.

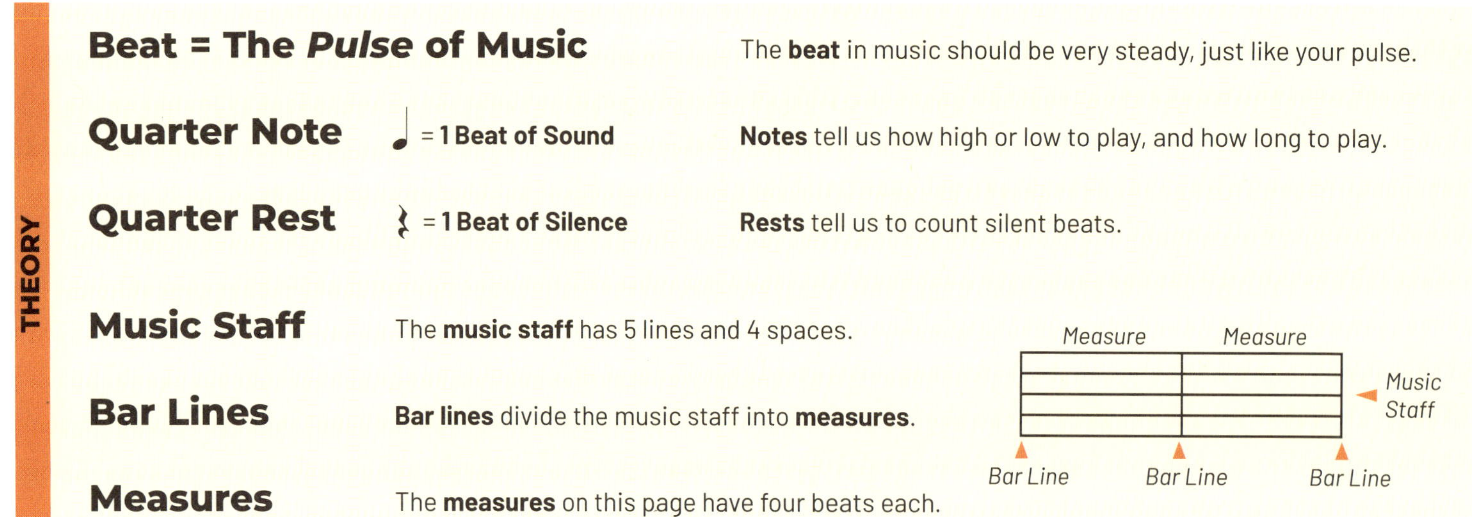

THEORY

Beat = The *Pulse* of Music — The **beat** in music should be very steady, just like your pulse.

Quarter Note ♩ = 1 Beat of Sound — **Notes** tell us how high or low to play, and how long to play.

Quarter Rest 𝄽 = 1 Beat of Silence — **Rests** tell us to count silent beats.

Music Staff — The **music staff** has 5 lines and 4 spaces.

Bar Lines — **Bar lines** divide the music staff into **measures**.

Measures — The **measures** on this page have four beats each.

1. TUNING TRACK *Wait quietly for your teacher to tune your instrument.*

2. LET'S PLAY "OPEN D"

Pizzicato (pizz.) ◄ *Pluck the strings*

0 ◄ *Open string*

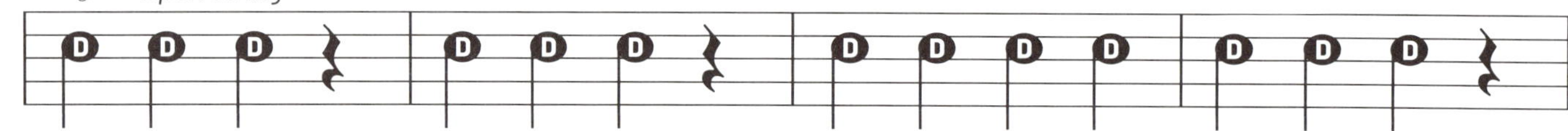

3. LET'S PLAY "OPEN A"

pizz.

0

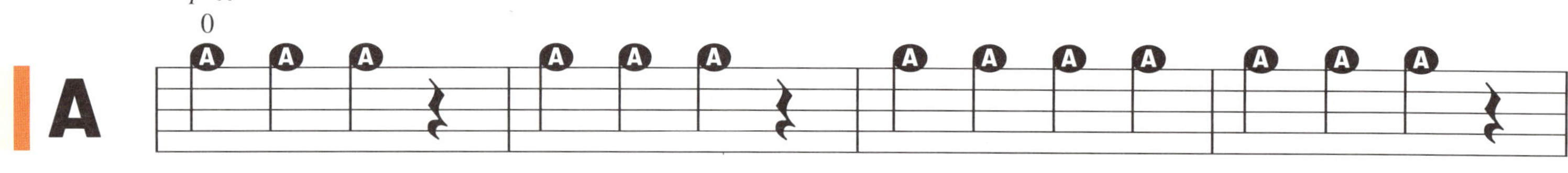

Keep a steady beat.

4. TWO'S A TEAM

pizz.

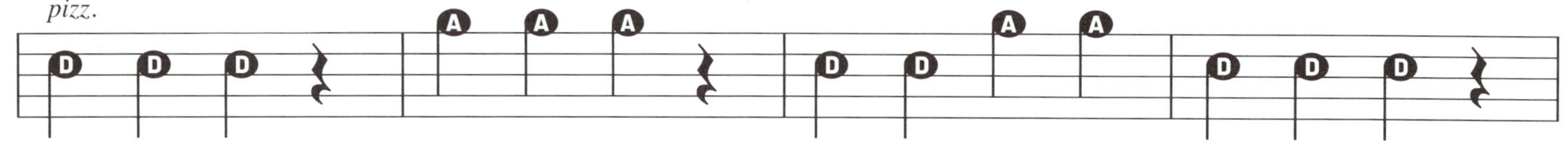

5. AT PIERROT'S DOOR *The melody is included on the online audio.*

pizz.

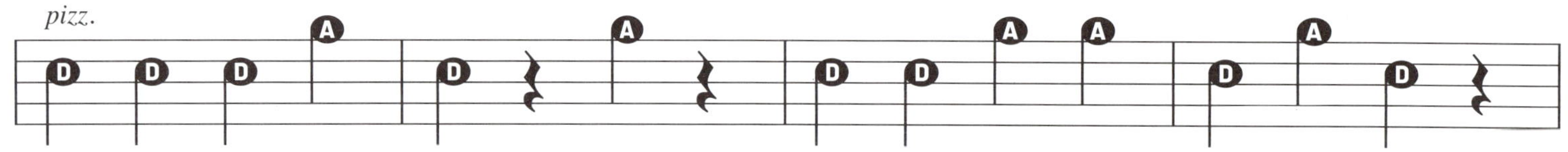

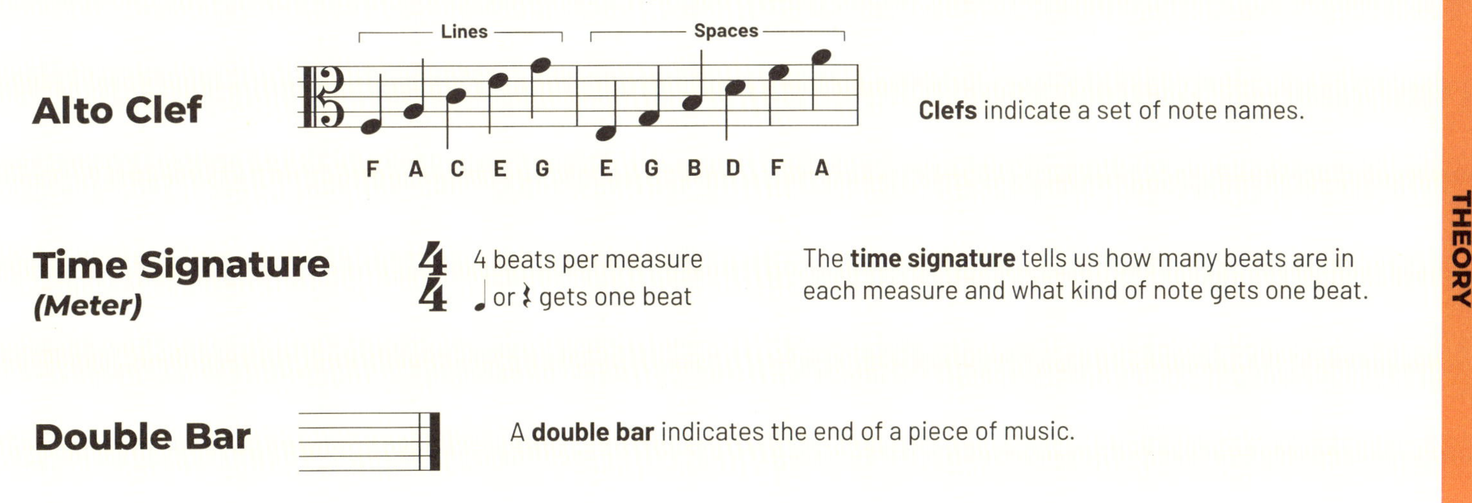

6. JUMPING JACKS *Identify the clef and time signature before playing.*

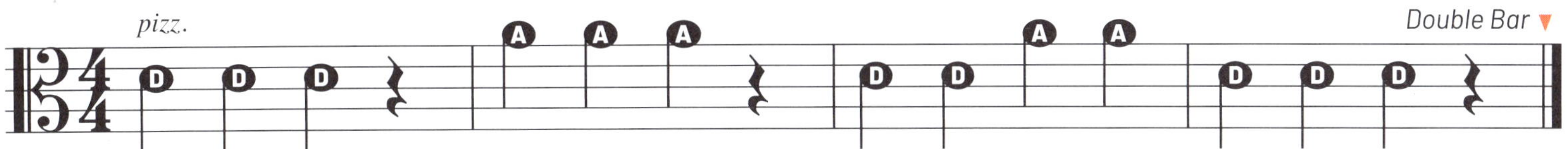

7. MIX 'EM UP

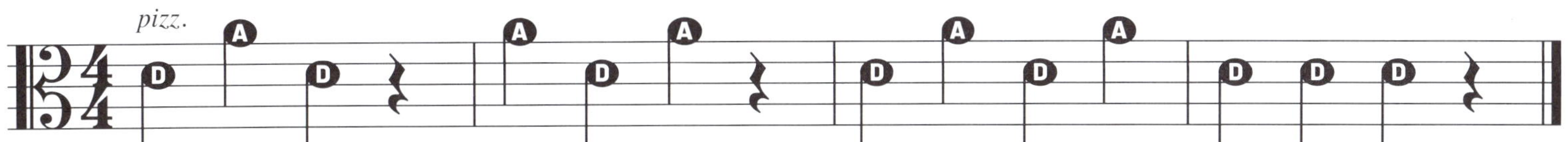

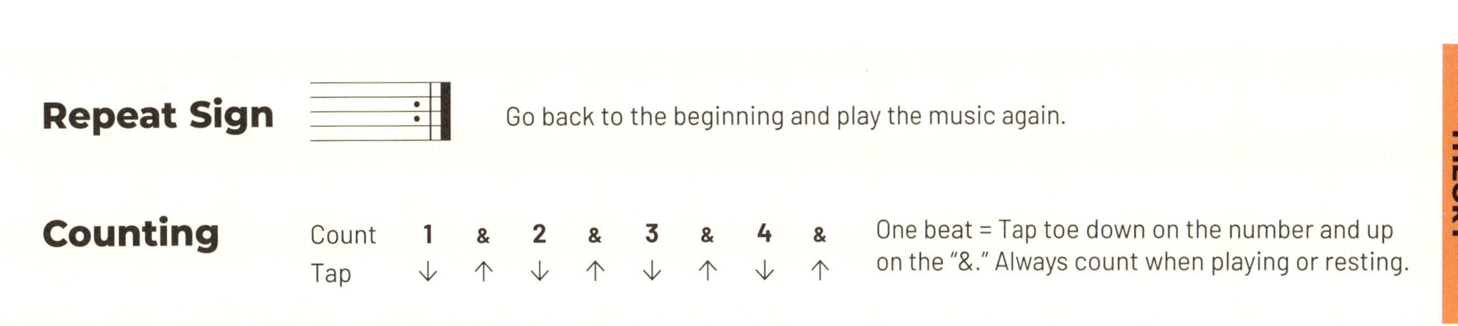

8. COUNT CAREFULLY *Keep a steady beat when playing or resting.*

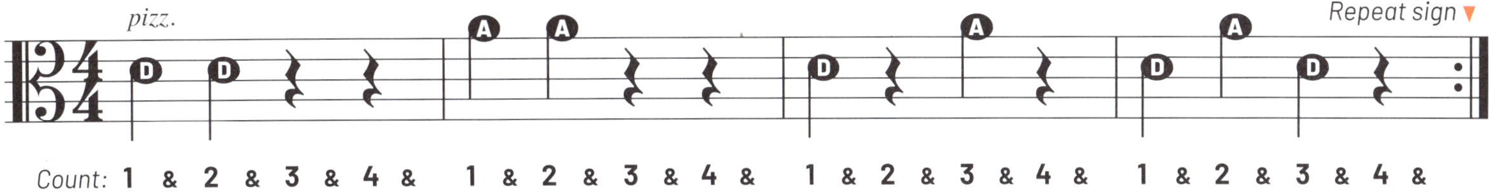

9. ESSENTIAL ELEMENTS QUIZ *Write in the counting before you play.*

SHAPING THE LEFT HAND

D STRING NOTES

Step 1 Shape your left hand as shown. Be certain your palm faces you.

0 = Open string
1 = 1st finger
2 = 2nd finger
3 = 3rd finger
4 = 4th finger

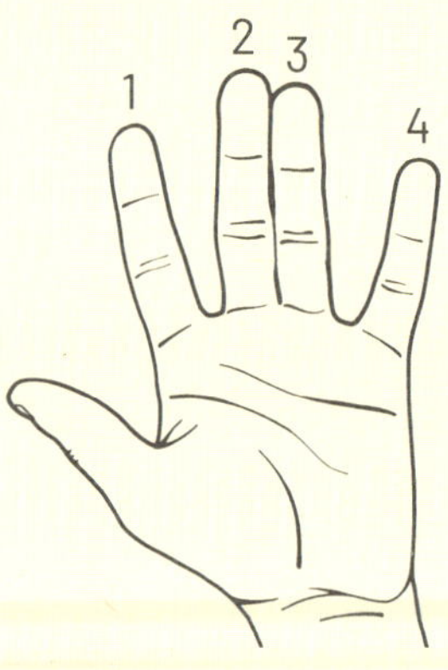

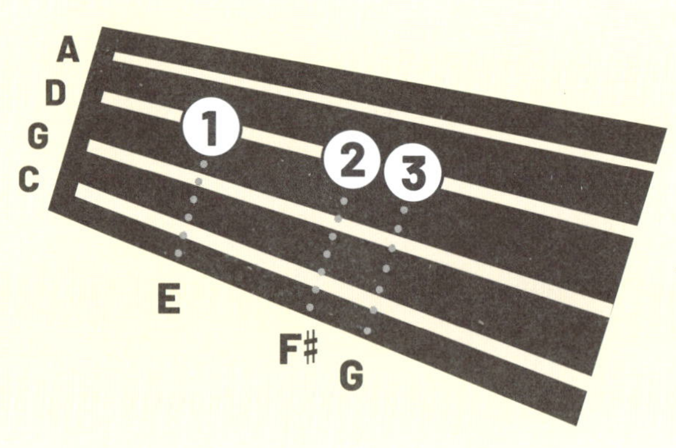

Step 2 Bring your hand to the fingerboard. Place your fingers on the D string, keeping your hand shaped as shown below. Be sure your 1st finger forms a square with the fingerboard, and your wrist is relaxed and straight.

G is played with 3 fingers on the D string.

F♯ is played with 2 fingers on the D string.

E is played with 1 finger on the D string.

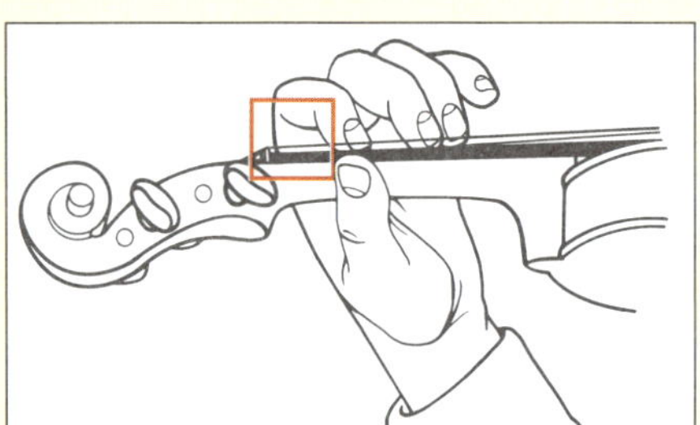

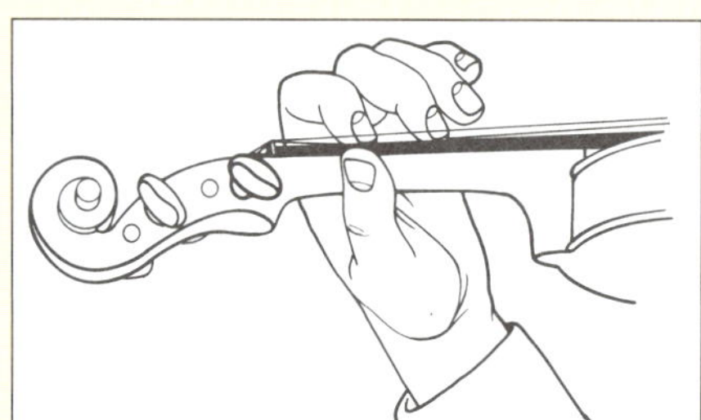

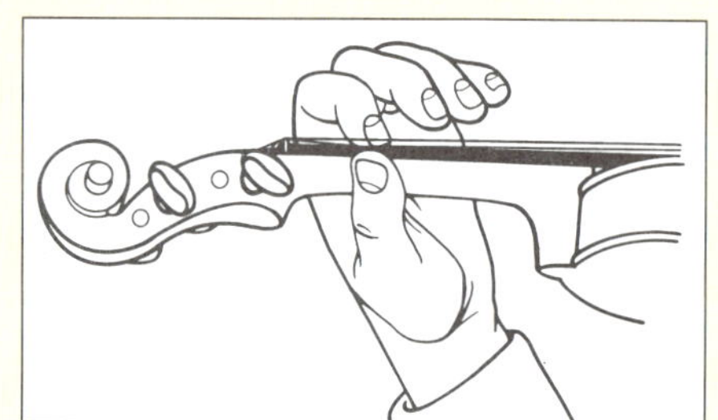

Listening Skills Play what your teacher plays. Listen carefully.

10. LET'S READ "G" *Start memorizing the note names.*

G

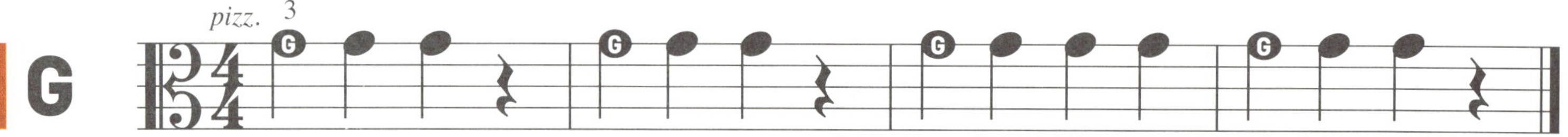

THEORY

Sharp ♯

A **sharp** sign raises the sound of notes and remains in effect for the entire measure. Notes without sharps are called **natural** notes.

11. LET'S READ "F♯" (F-sharp)

F♯

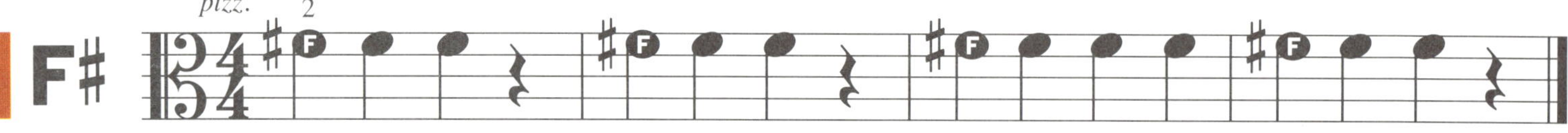

▲ *Play all F♯'s. Sharps apply to the entire measure.*

12. LIFT OFF

✔ Is your left hand shaped as shown in the diagrams above?

SHAPING THE RIGHT HAND

BOW BUILDER ONE

Pencil Hold

Step 1 Hold a pencil in your left hand at eye level.

Step 2 Hang your right fingers over the top of the pencil, as shown.

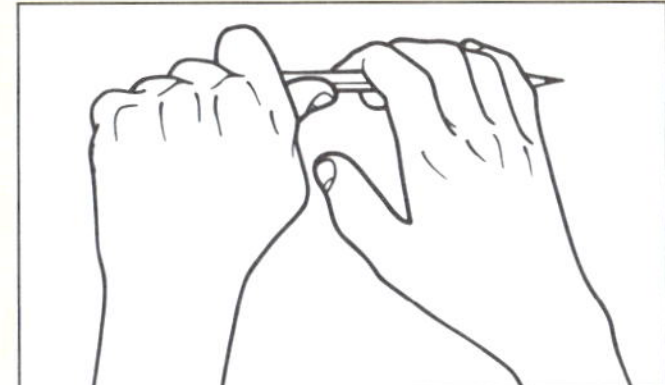

Step 3 Place your right 4th finger on top of the pencil.

Step 4 Touch the tip of your right thumb to the pencil just opposite your 2nd finger. The curve of your thumb will form an oval with the finger.

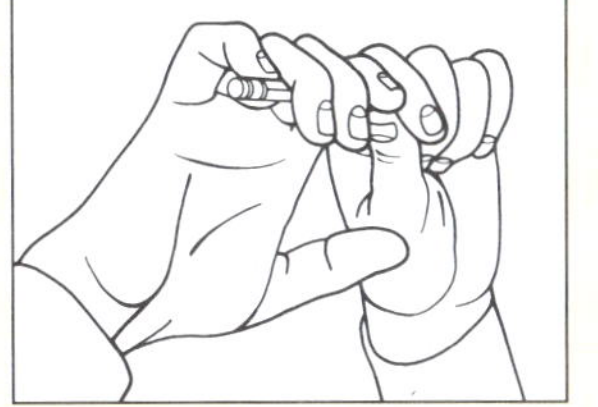

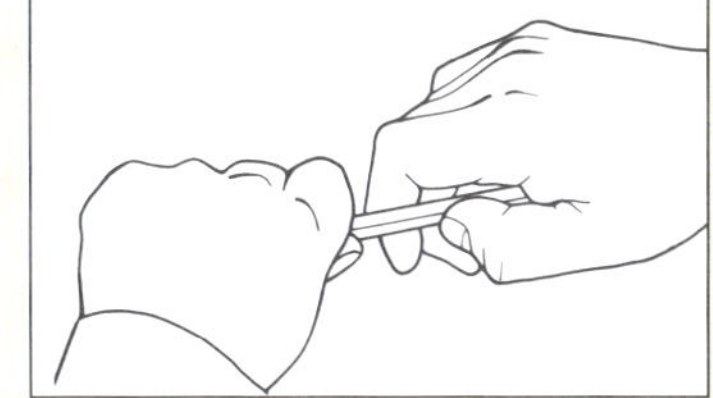

Step 5 Lean your right hand so the first finger rests on top of the pencil between the 1st and 2nd joints. Keep your fingers relaxed. Remove your left hand from the pencil. Practice shaping your hand on the pencil until it feels natural to you.

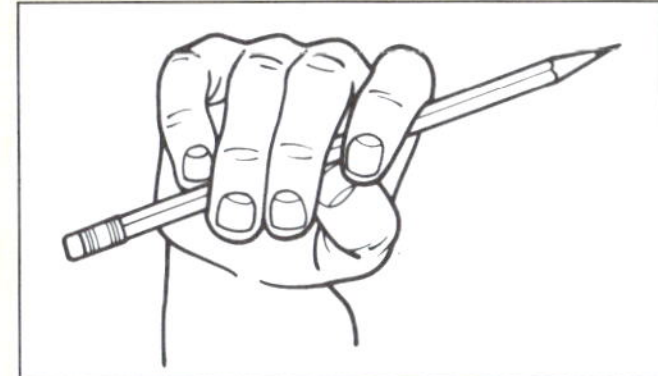

 Practice BOW BUILDER ONE daily.

13. ON THE TRAIL *Say or sing the note names before you play.*

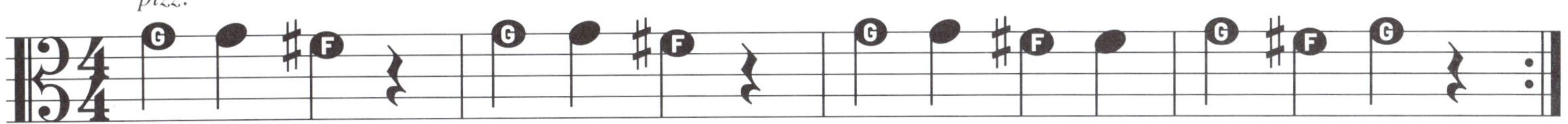

14. LET'S READ "E"

E

15. WALKING SONG

16. ESSENTIAL ELEMENTS QUIZ *Draw the missing symbols where they belong before you play:*

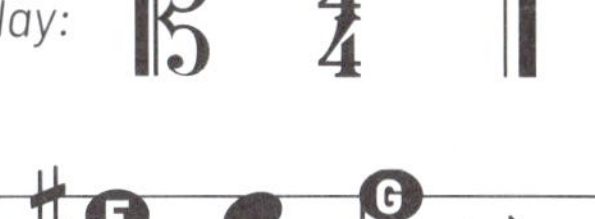

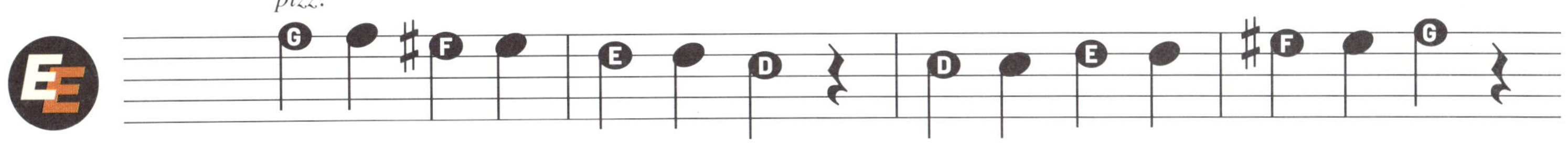

BOW BUILDER TWO

Pencil Hold Exercises

I'm Outta Here
Wave good-bye while keeping your wrist relaxed.

Thumb Flexers
Flex your thumb in and out.

Finger Taps
Tap your first finger. Then tap your fourth finger.

Knuckle Turnovers
Turn your hand over and be sure your thumb knuckle is bent, as shown.

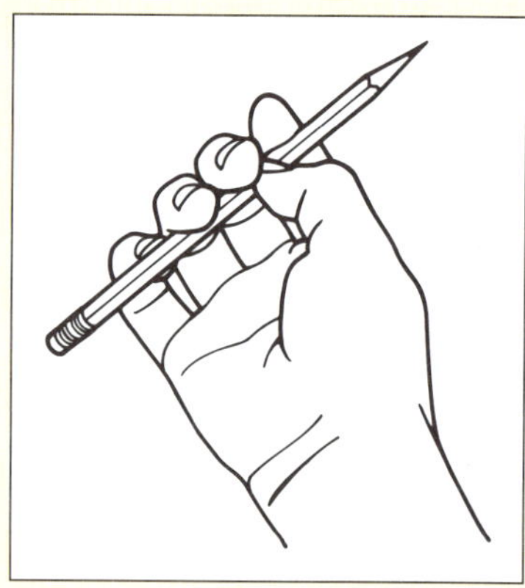

Knuckle Turnovers

BOW BUILDER THREE

Bowing Motions

Swingin' Out
Put one finger inside your right elbow and swing your arm as shown.

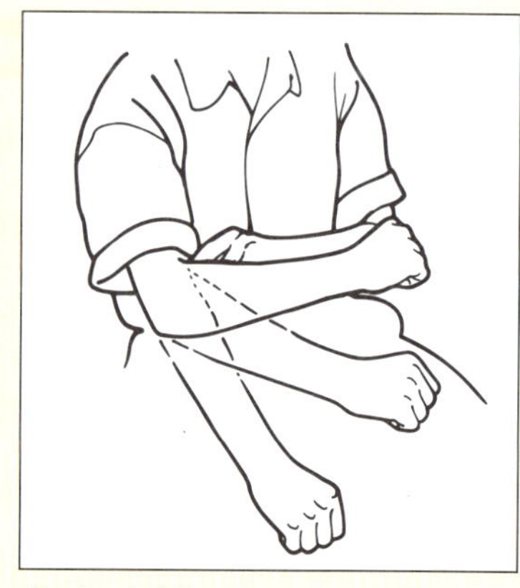

Swingin' Out

17. HOP SCOTCH

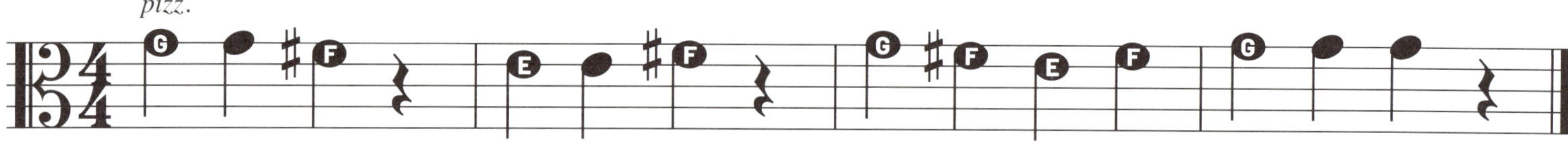

Count: 1 & 2 & 3 & 4 & 1 & 2 & 3 & 4 & 1 & 2 & 3 & 4 & 1 & 2 & 3 & 4 &

HISTORY

Folk songs have been an important part of cultures for centuries and have been passed on from generation to generation. Folk song melodies help define the sound of a culture or region. This folk song comes from the Slavic region of eastern Europe.

18. MORNING DANCE

Slavic Folk Song

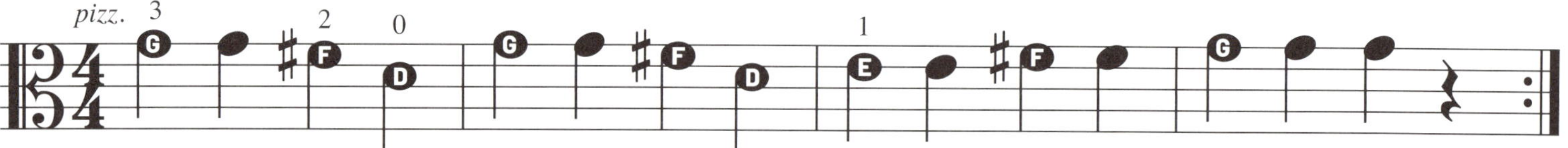

19. ROLLING ALONG

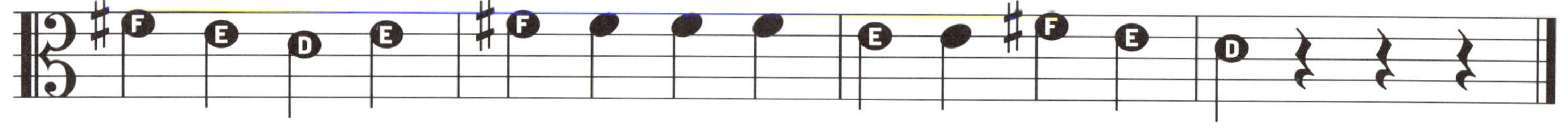

WORKOUTS

Place your instrument in shoulder position as shown on page 3. Then practice the following exercises with your left hand.

Finger Taps

Tap fingertips on any string. Practice in different combinations of fingers.

Pull Aways

Pull your left hand away from the side of the neck, while keeping the thumb and fingers on the instrument.

Strummin' Along

Strum the strings with your 4th finger while swinging your elbow under the viola, as shown.

Strummin' Along

20. GOOD KING WENCESLAS

Welsh Folk Song

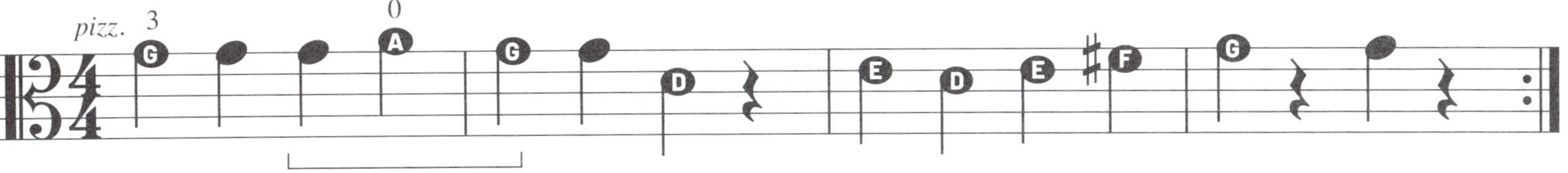

▲ *Keep fingers down when you see this bracket.*

21. SEMINOLE CHANT

Count: 1 & 2 & 3 & 4 & 1 & 2 & 3 & 4 & 1 & 2 & 3 & 4 & 1 & 2 & 3 & 4 &

22. ESSENTIAL ELEMENTS QUIZ – LIGHTLY ROW

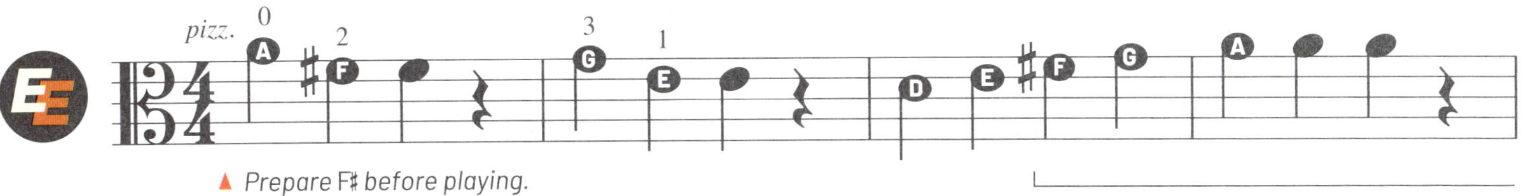

▲ *Prepare F♯ before playing.*

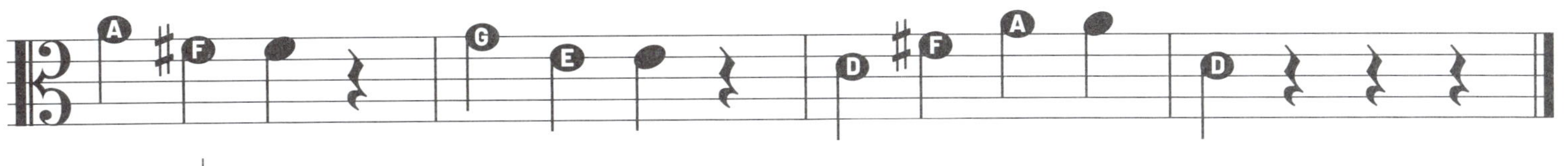

A STRING NOTES

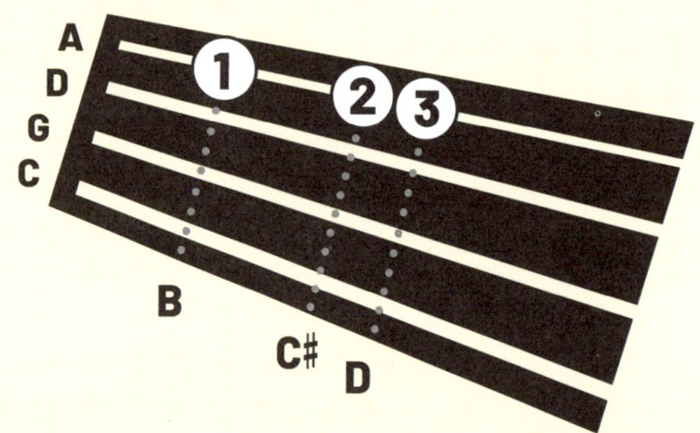

D is played with 3 fingers on the A string.

C♯ is played with 2 fingers on the A string.

B is played with 1 finger on the A string.

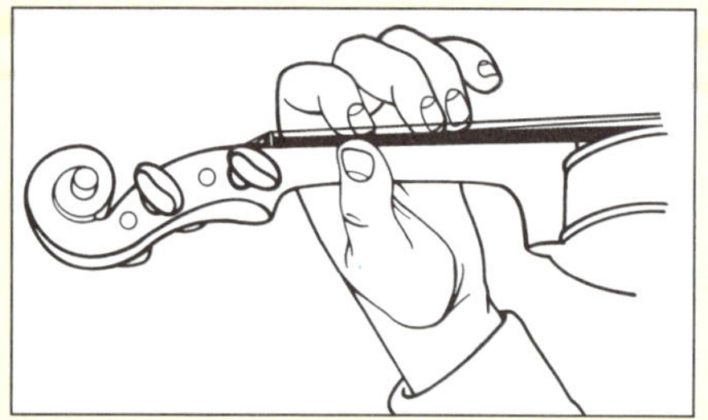

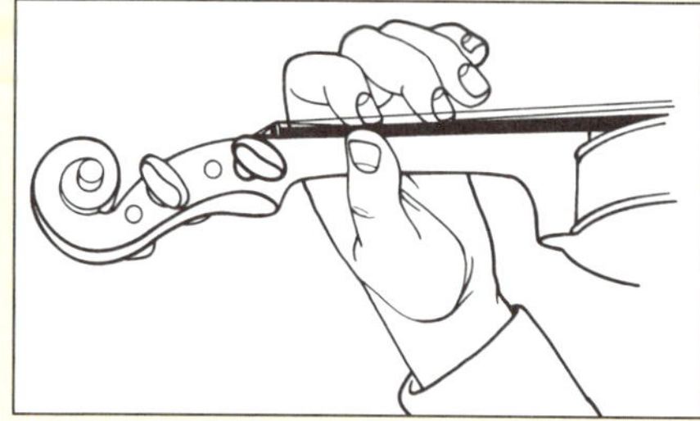

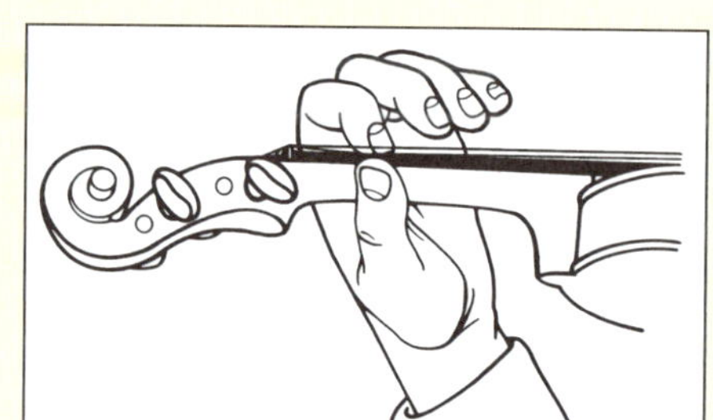

Play what your teacher plays. Listen carefully.

THEORY

Ledger Lines

Ledger lines extend the music staff higher or lower.

23. LET'S READ "D"

24. LET'S READ "C♯" (C-sharp)

▲ *Play all C♯'s. Sharps apply to the entire measure.*

25. TAKE OFF

26. CARIBBEAN ISLAND

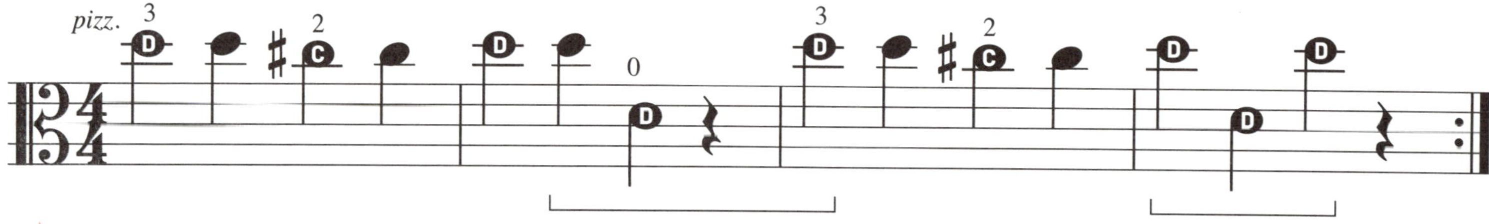

★ Practice BOW BUILDERS ONE, TWO, and THREE daily.

27. OLYMPIC HIGH JUMP

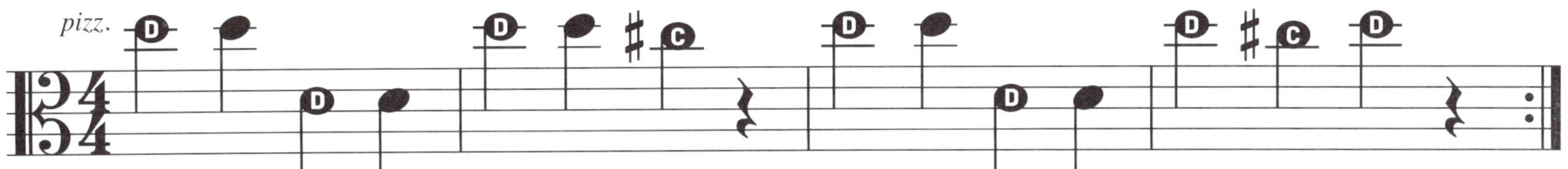

28. LET'S READ "B"

B

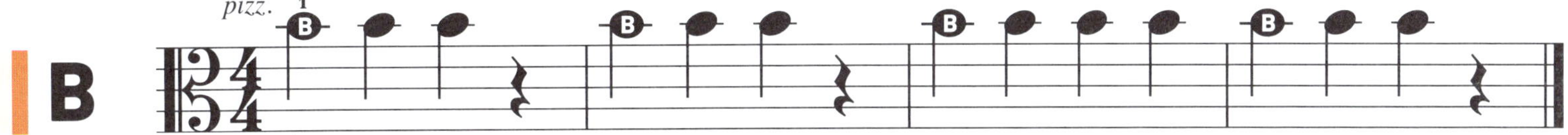

29. HALF WAY DOWN

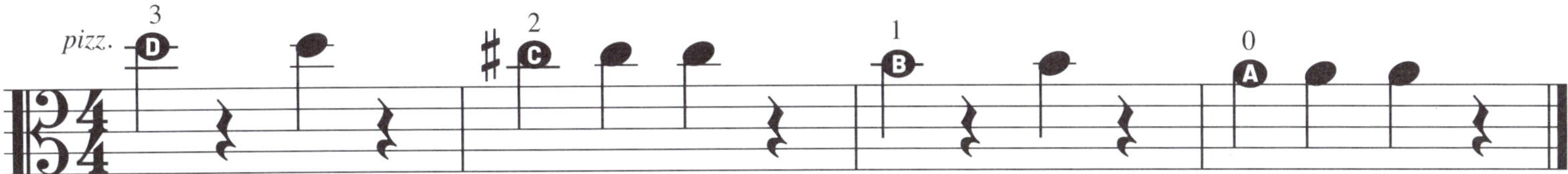

30. RIGHT BACK UP

Scale A **scale** is a sequence of notes in ascending or descending order. Like a musical "ladder," each note is the next consecutive step of the scale. This is your D Scale. The first and last notes are both D.

31. DOWN THE D SCALE *Remember to memorize the note names.*

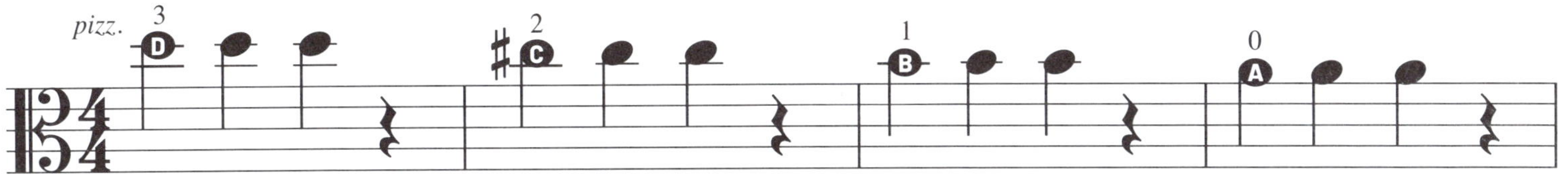

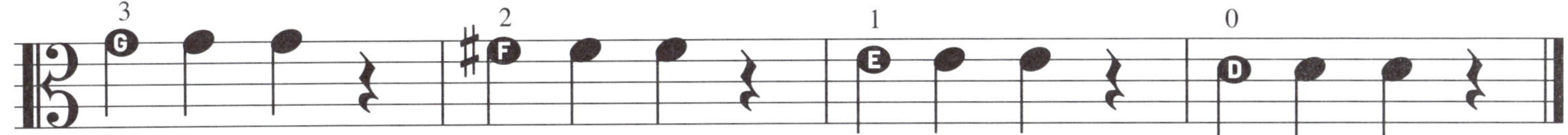

32. ESSENTIAL ELEMENTS QUIZ – UP THE D SCALE

BOW BUILDER FOUR

On the Bow (Early Bow Hold)

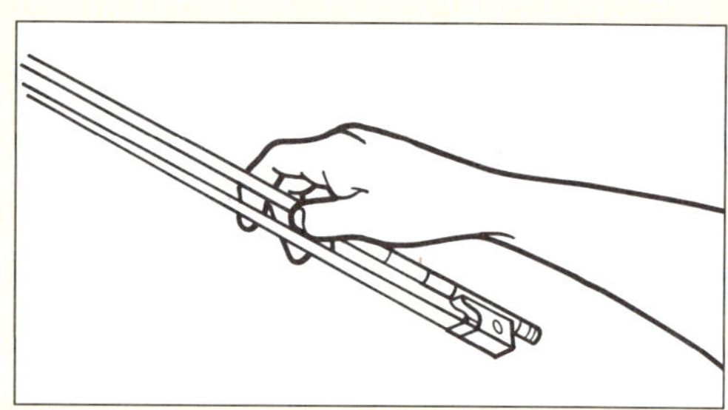

Balancing The Bow

Step 1 Identify all parts of the bow (see page 2). Hold the bow in your left hand near the tip with the frog pointing to the right.

Step 2 Put your right thumb and 2nd finger on the bow stick near the middle of the bow.

Step 3 Shape your right hand on the bow stick, as shown.

Step 4 Turn your right hand over, and be sure your thumb and fingers are curved.

Step 5 Hold the bow and repeat the exercises on page 8.

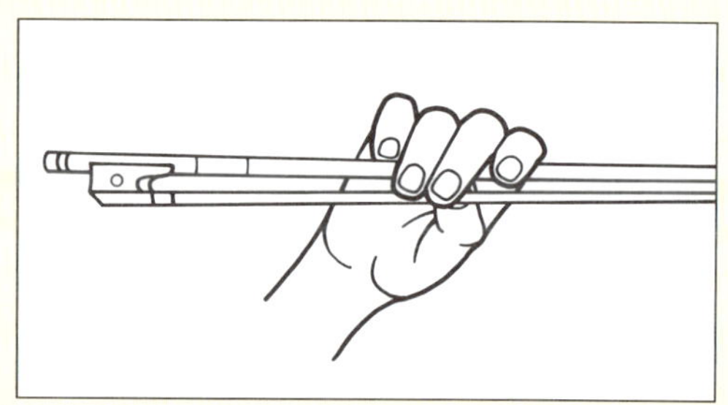

Early Bow Hold

Alert Do not place your bow on the instrument until instructed to do so by your teacher.

33. SONG FOR CHRISTINE

34. NATALIE'S ROSE *Remember to count.*

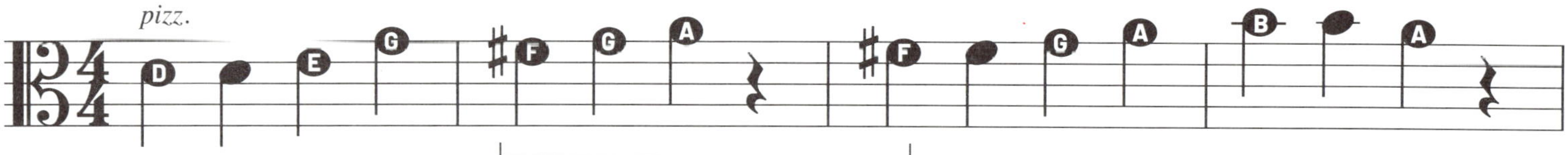

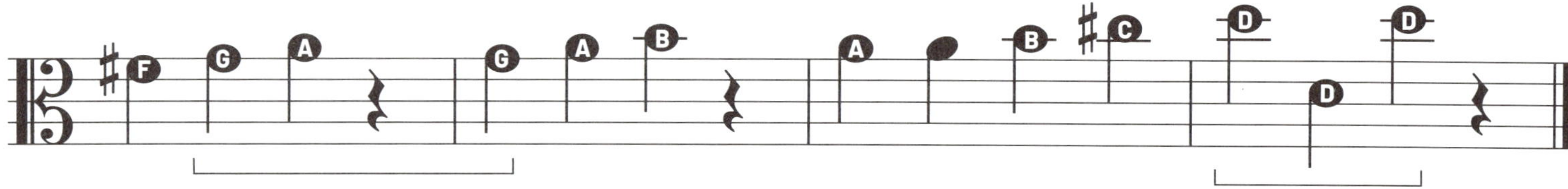

35. ESSENTIAL CREATIVITY *How many words can you create by drawing notes on the staff below?*

Example **E G G**

Folk songs often tell stories. This **Israeli folk song** describes a game played with a dreidel, a small table-top spinning toy that has been enjoyed by families for centuries. The game is especially popular in December around the time of Hanukkah.

36. DREIDEL

Israeli Folk Song

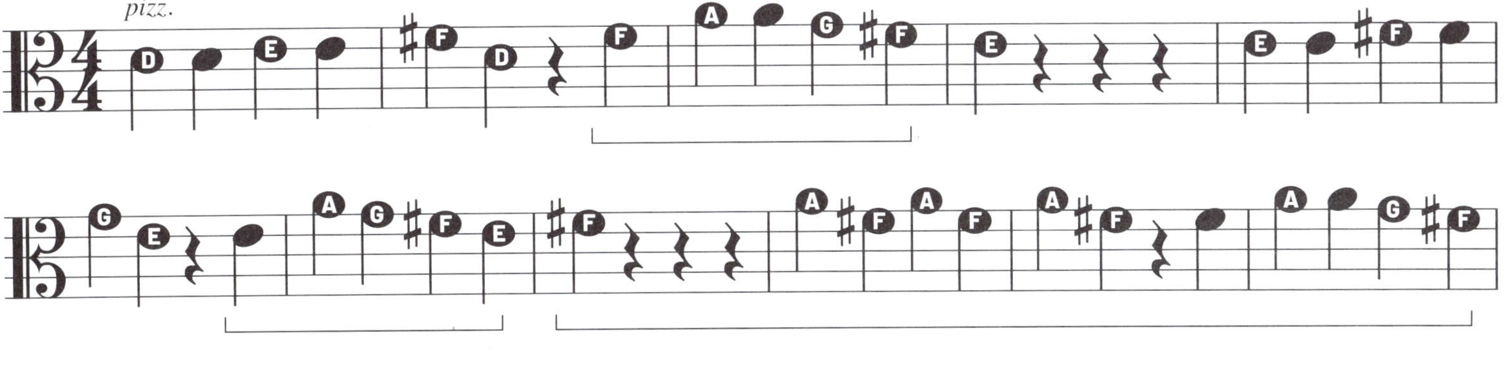

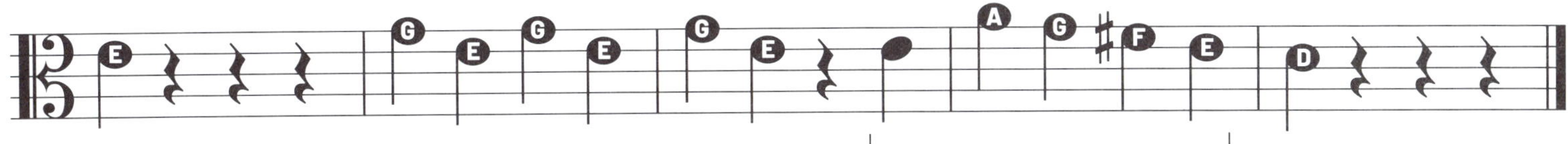

BOW BUILDER FIVE

Shadow Bowing

Shadow Bowing is bowing without the instrument.

Step 1 Tighten the bow hair as instructed by your teacher.

Step 2 Place the rosin in your left hand. Hold the bow at the balance point.

Step 3 Shadow bow by slowly moving the bow back and forth on the rosin. Be sure to move the bow, not the rosin.

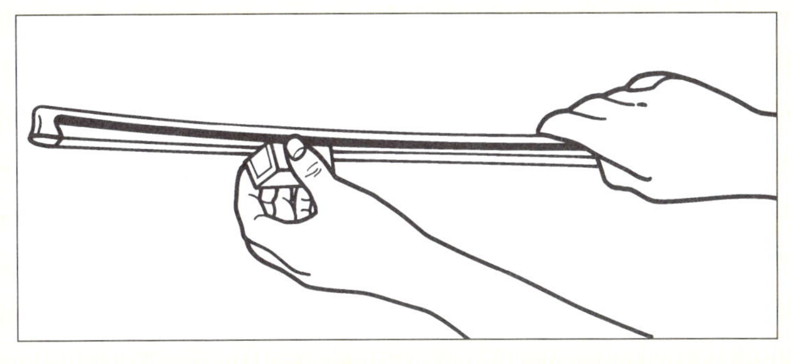

Down Bow ⊓ Move the bow away from your body (to the right).

Up Bow V Move the bow toward your body (to the left).

37. ROSIN RAP #1 *Bow these exercises on the rosin.*

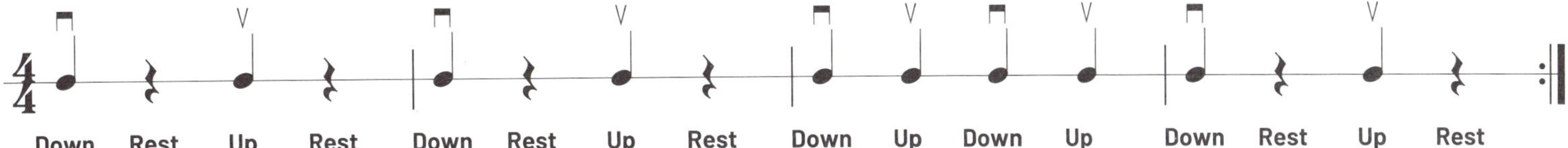

38. ROSIN RAP #2

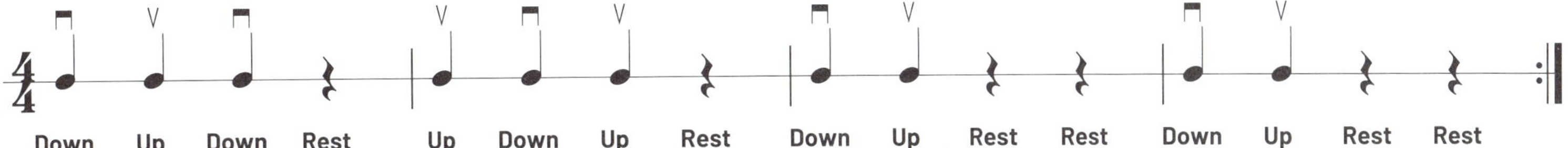

39. ROSIN RAP #3

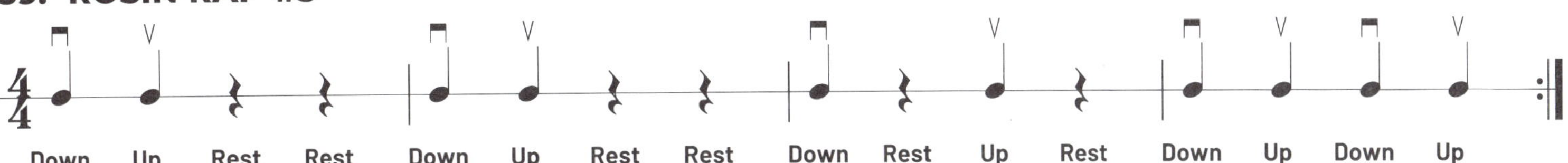

✔ Is your bow hand shaped as shown in the diagram above?

THEORY

Review these notes. Write the letter names in the spaces below.

40. CAROLINA BREEZE

41. JINGLE BELLS

J. S. Pierpont

42. OLD MACDONALD HAD A FARM

American Folk Song

★ Practice BOW BUILDER FIVE daily.

Austrian composer **Wolfgang Amadeus Mozart** (1756–1791) was a child prodigy who first performed in concert at age 6. He lived during the time of the American Revolution (1775–1783). Mozart's music is melodic and imaginative. He wrote hundreds of compositions, including a piano piece based on this familiar song.

43. A MOZART MELODY

Adapted by W. A. Mozart

THEORY

Key Signature D MAJOR

A **key signature** tells us what notes to play with sharps and flats throughout the entire piece. Play all F's as F♯ (F-sharp) and all C's as C♯ (C-sharp) when you see this key signature, which is called "D Major."

44. MATTHEW'S MARCH

▲ *Play F♯'s and C♯'s when you see this key signature.*

45. CHRISTOPHER'S TUNE

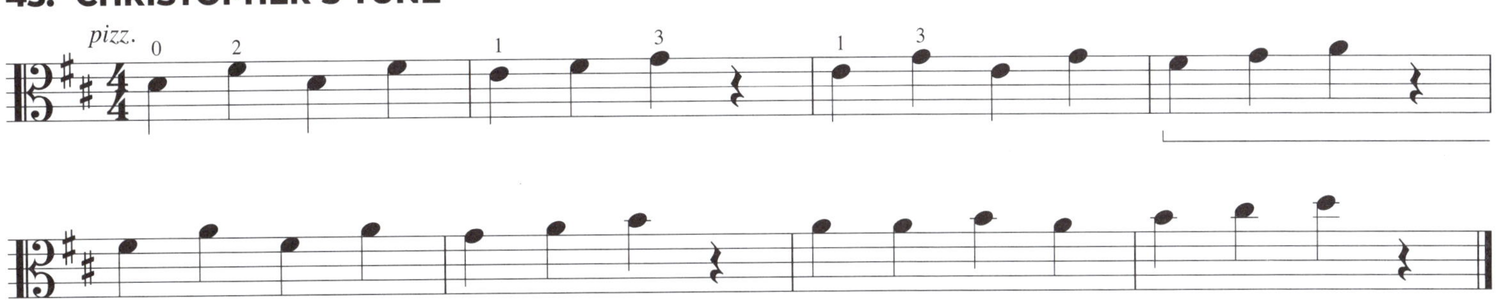

46. ESSENTIAL CREATIVITY

Play the notes below. Then compose your own music for the last two measures using the notes you have learned with this rhythm:

BOW BUILDER SIX

Let's Bow!

Early Bow Hold

Regular Bow Hold

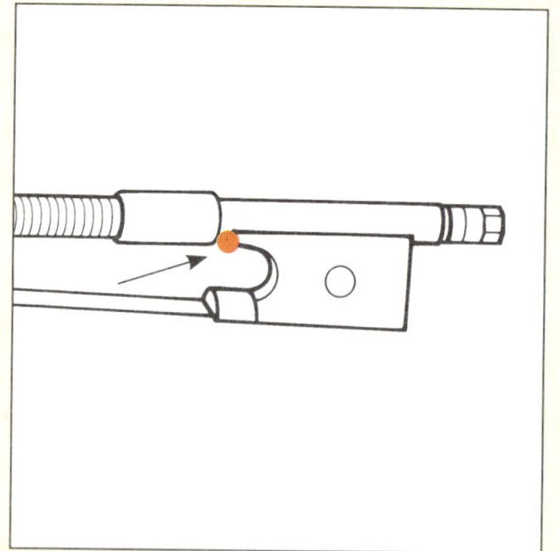

Thumb Placement

Step 1 Hold the instrument with your left hand on the upper bout, as illustrated.

Step 2 Hold the bow at the balance point (Early Bow Hold). Your right elbow should be slightly lower than your hand.

Your teacher will suggest when to begin moving your bow hand toward the frog, as shown in the Regular Bow Hold illustration. The tip of your thumb will move to the place on the stick where it touches the frog.

Listening Skills

Play what your teacher plays. Listen carefully. Your tone should be smooth and even.

47. BOW ON THE D STRING

arco ◄ *Play with the bow on the string.*

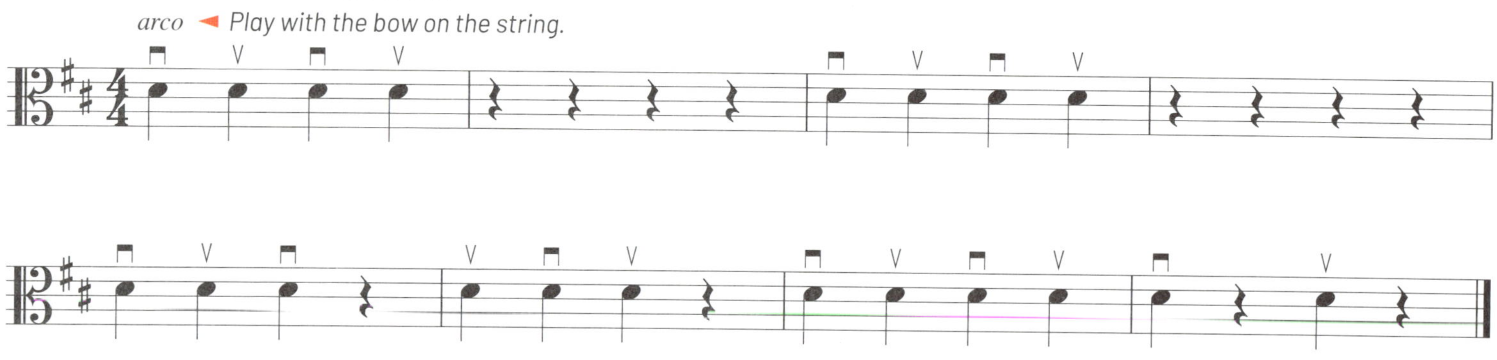

48. BOW ON THE A STRING

WORKOUTS

String Levels

Your arm moves when bowing on different strings. Memorize these guidelines:

- **Raise** your arm to play **lower**-pitched strings.
- **Lower** your arm to play **higher**-pitched strings.

Raise arm = lower string

Lower arm = higher string

49. RAISE AND LOWER

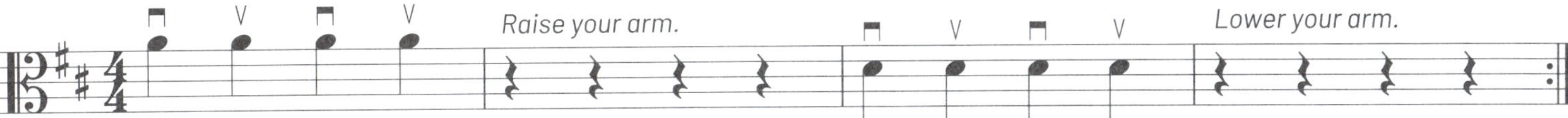

50. TEETER TOTTER

51. MIRROR IMAGE

Bow Lift

, Lift the bow and return to its starting point.

52. A STRAND OF D 'N' A

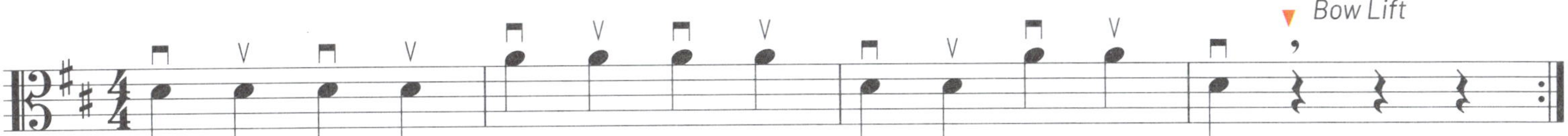

53. ESSENTIAL ELEMENTS QUIZ – OLYMPIC CHALLENGE

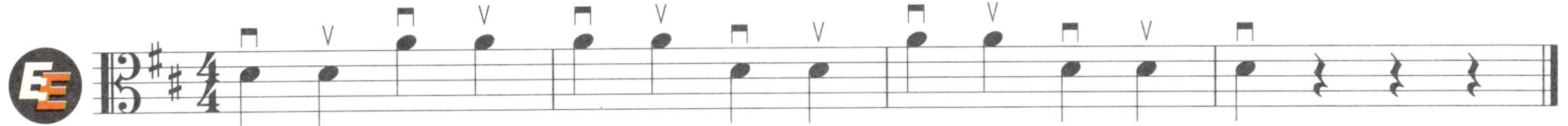

BOW BUILDER SEVEN

Combining Both Hands

Using notes from the D major scale, echo what your teacher plays.

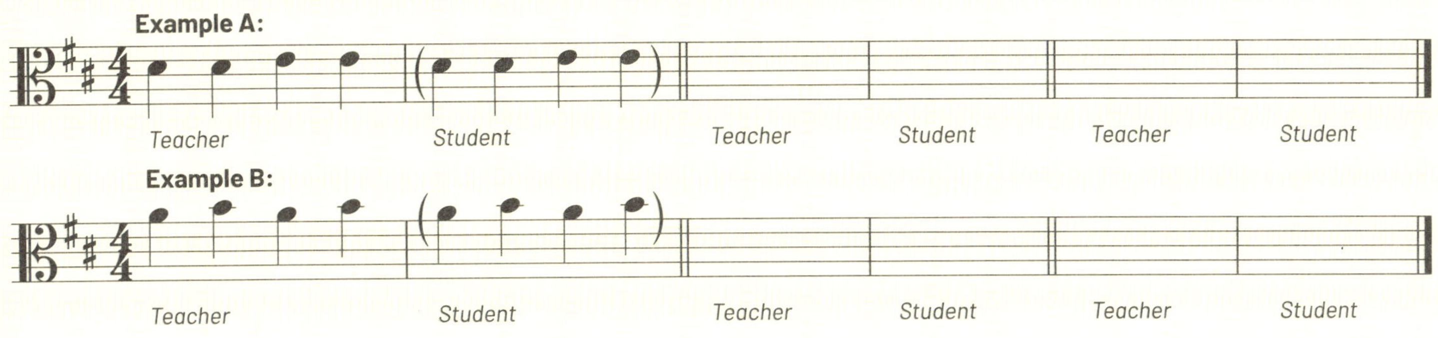

PUTTING IT ALL TOGETHER

Congratulations! You are now ready to practice like an advanced player by combining left and right hand skills while reading music. When learning a new line of music, follow these steps for success:

Step 1 Tap your toe and say or sing the letter names.

Step 2 Play *pizz.* and say or sing the letter names.

Step 3 Shadow bow and say or sing the letter names.

Step 4 Bow and play as written.

54. BOWING "G"

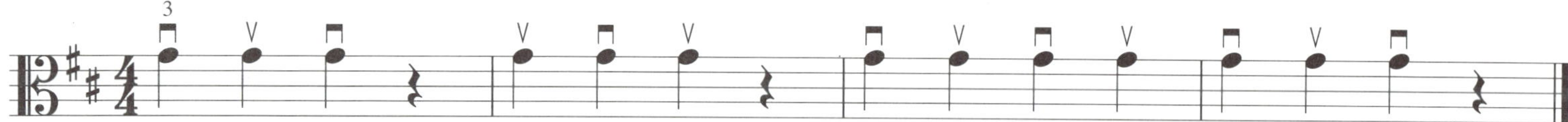

55. BACK AND FORTH

56. DOWN AND UP

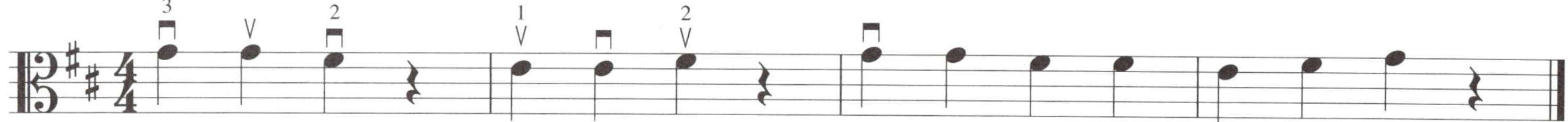

57. TRIBAL LAMENT

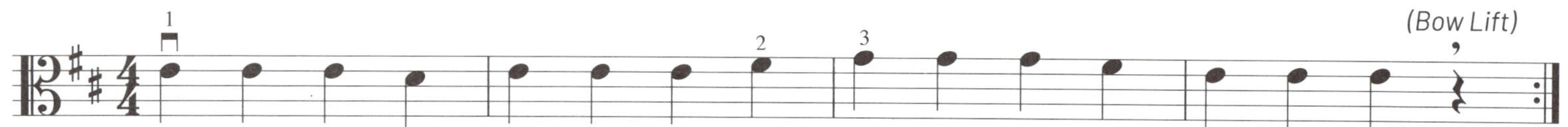

58. BOWING "D"

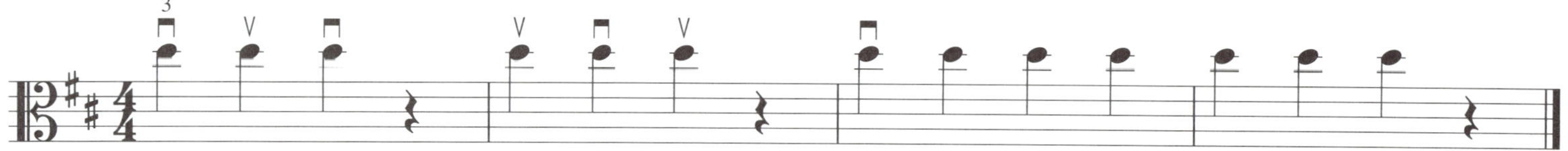

59. LITTLE STEPS

60. ELEVATOR DOWN

61. ELEVATOR UP

62. DOWN THE D MAJOR SCALE

63. SCALE SIMULATOR *Remember to count.*

64. ESSENTIAL ELEMENTS QUIZ – THE D MAJOR SCALE

Special Viola Exercise

While the basses learn a new note, draw the bar lines in the music below. Then write in the counting.

65. LET'S READ "C♯" – Review

THEORY

Eighth Notes

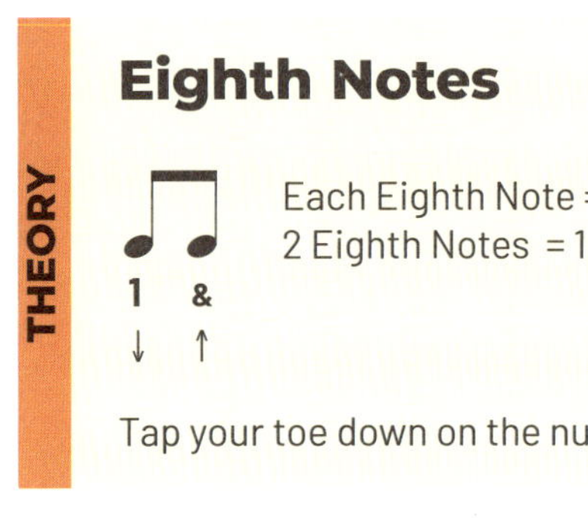

Each Eighth Note = 1/2 Beat
2 Eighth Notes = 1 Beat

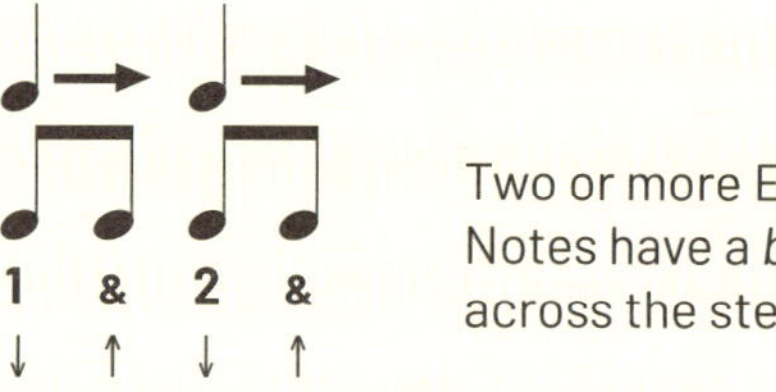

Two or more Eighth Notes have a *beam* across the stems.

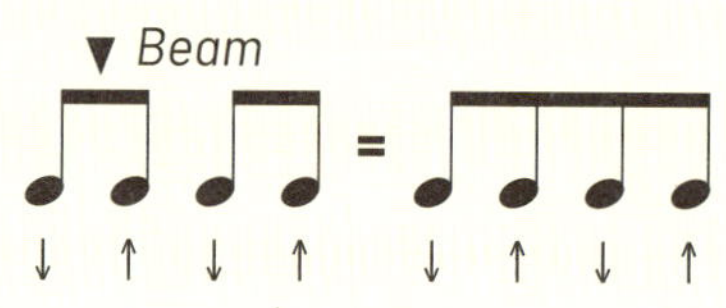

Tap your toe down on the number and up on the "&."

66. RHYTHM RAP

Shadow bow and count before playing.

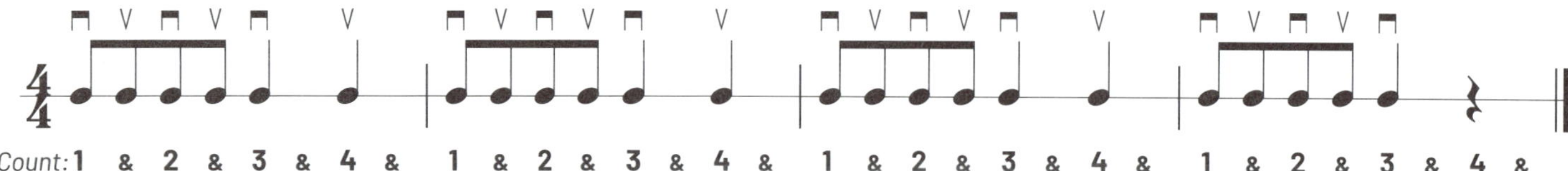

67. PEPPERONI PIZZA

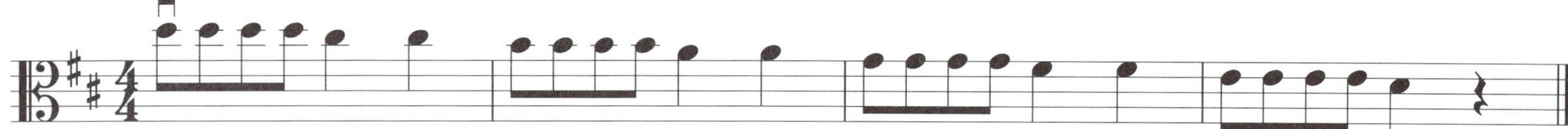

68. RHYTHM RAP

Shadow bow and count before playing.

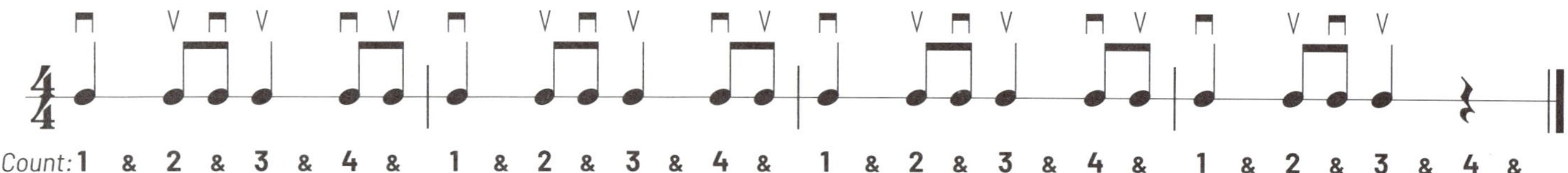

69. D MAJOR SCALE UP

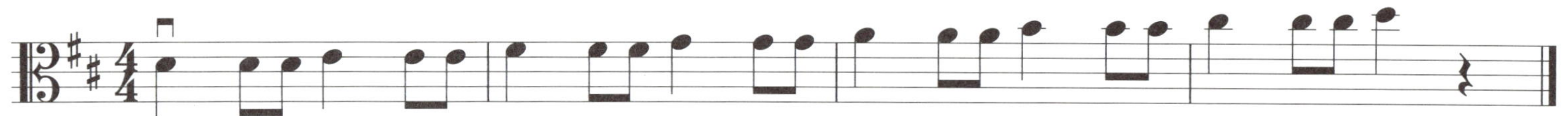

Tempo Markings

Tempo is the speed of music. Tempo markings are usually written above the staff, in Italian.

Allegro – Fast tempo **Moderato** – Medium tempo **Andante** – Slower, walking tempo

70. HOT CROSS BUNS

Moderato

71. AU CLAIRE DE LA LUNE

French Folk Song

Andante

72. RHYTHM RAP

Shadow bow and count before playing.

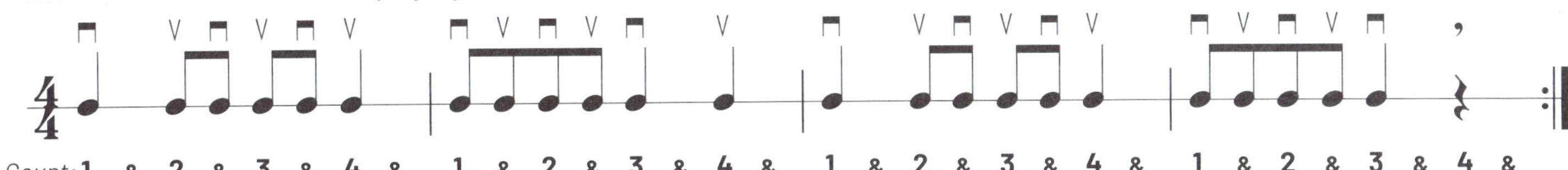

73. BUCKEYE SALUTE

Moderato

Time Signature

= **2 beats** per measure
= **Quarter** note gets one beat

Conducting

Practice conducting this two-beat pattern.

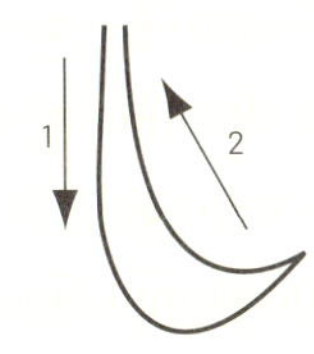

THEORY

74. RHYTHM RAP

Shadow bow and count before playing.

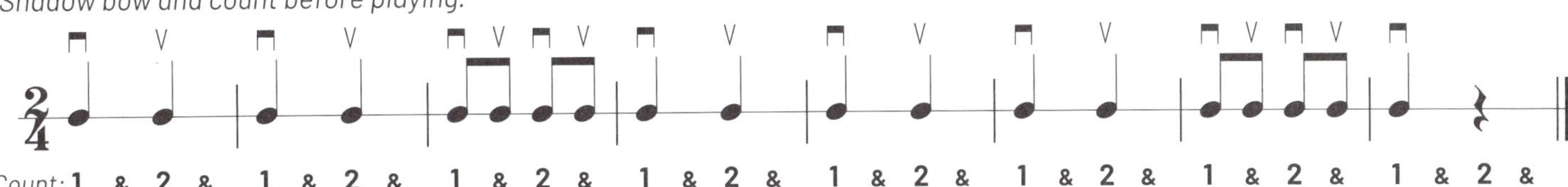

75. TWO BY TWO

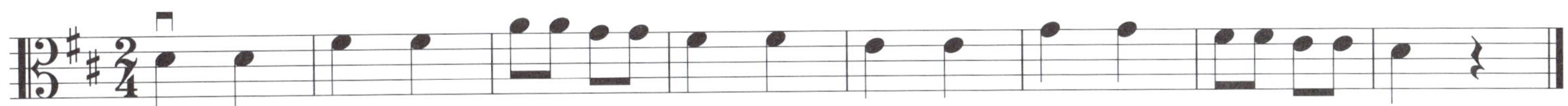

1st & 2nd Endings

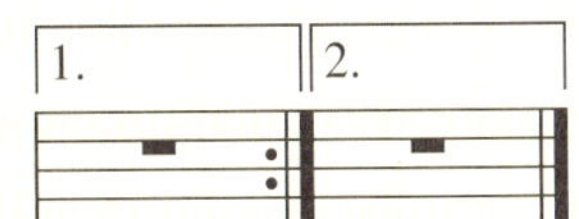

Play the 1st ending the 1st time through. Then, repeat the same section of music, skip the 1st ending, and play the 2nd ending.

THEORY

76. ESSENTIAL ELEMENTS QUIZ – FOR PETE'S SAKE

Moderato

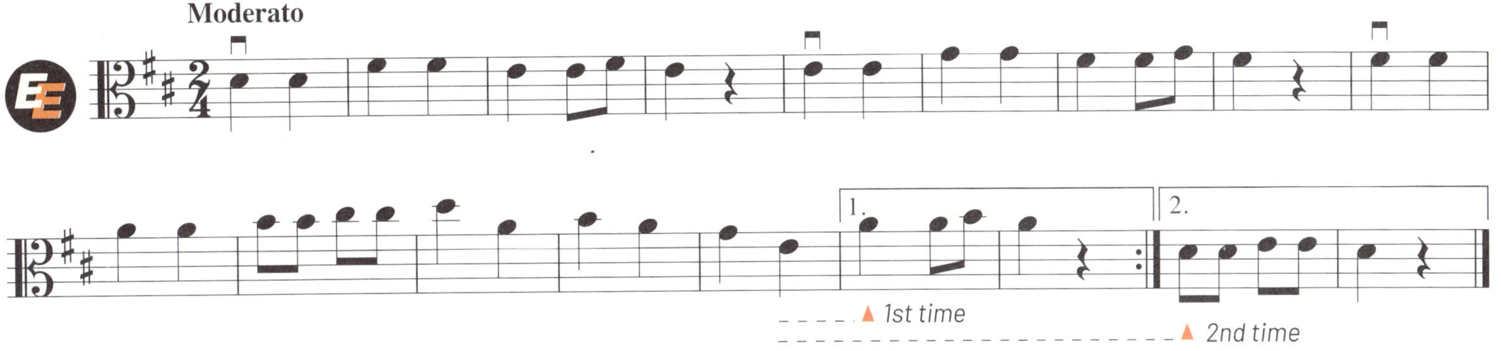

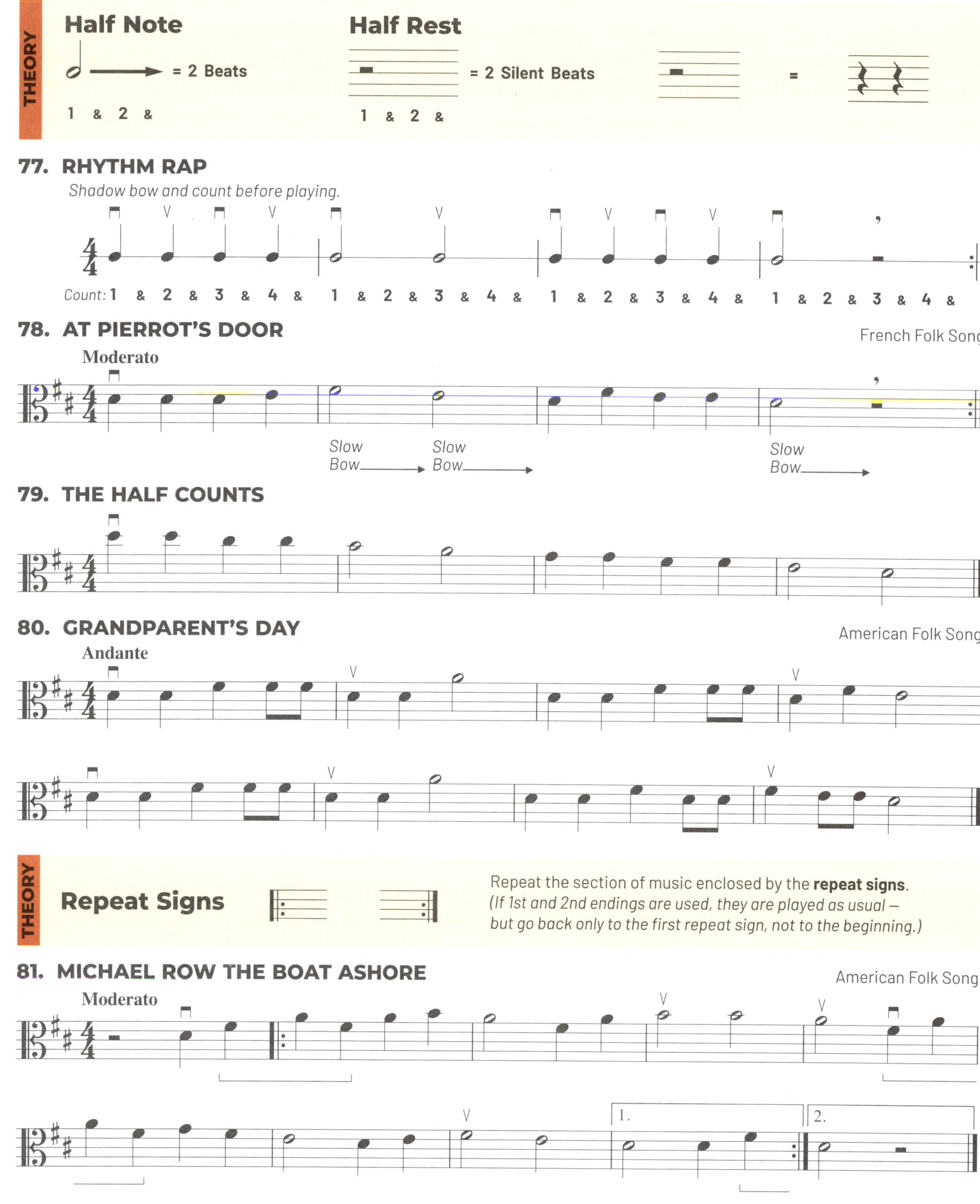

Looking for some more fun music to play?
See the inside front cover for instructions on accessing recent popular Bonus Songs.

4TH FINGER

Your **4th finger** is often used to match the pitch of the next highest open string, creating a smoother tone and fewer changes between the strings for bowing.

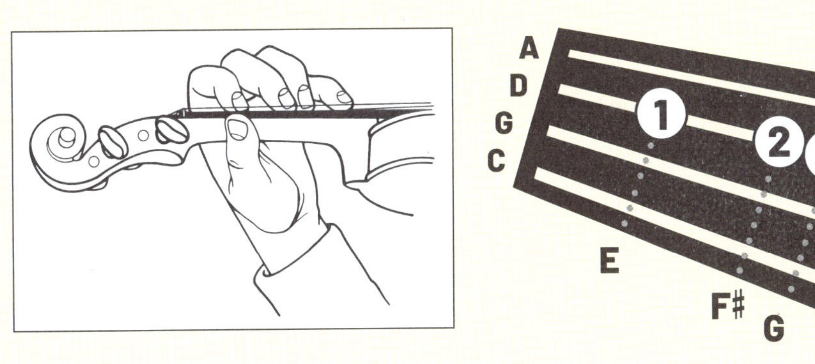

83. FOUR BY FOUR

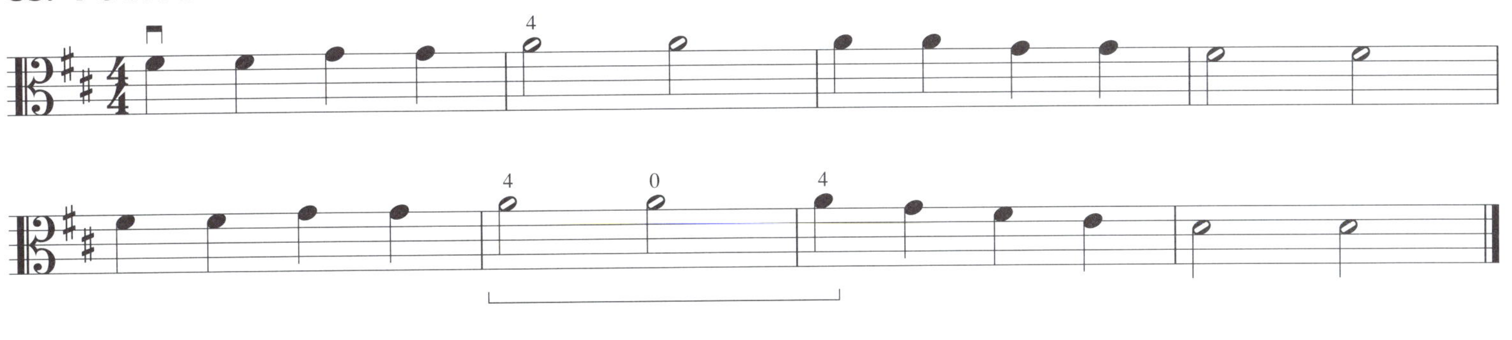

84. 4TH FINGER MARATHON

85. HIGH FLYING

German composer **Ludwig van Beethoven** (1770–1827) was one of the world's greatest composers. He was completely deaf by 1802. Although he could not hear music like we do, he could "hear" it in his mind. The theme of his final *Symphony No. 9* is called "Ode To Joy," and was written to the text of a poem by Friedrich von Schiller. "Ode To Joy" was featured in concerts celebrating the reunification of Germany in 1990.

HISTORY

86. ESSENTIAL ELEMENTS QUIZ – ODE TO JOY

Ludwig van Beethoven

PERFORMANCE SPOTLIGHT

Good performers are on time with their instruments and music ready, dressed appropriately, and know their music well.

87. SCALE WARM-UP

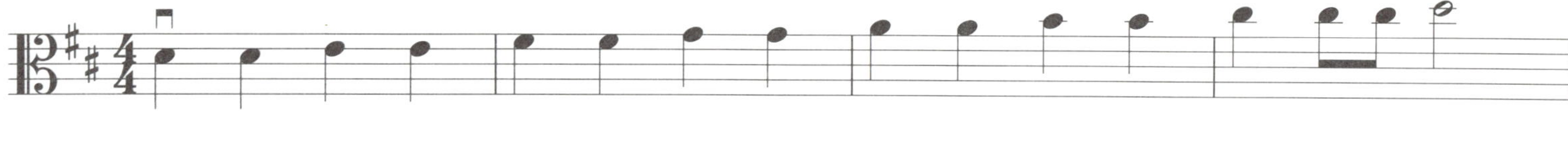

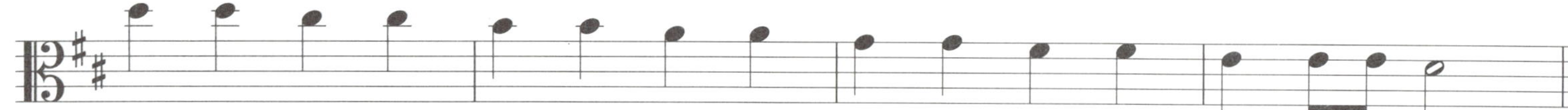

88. FRÈRE JACQUES – Round *(When group A reaches ②, group B begins at ①)*

French Folk Song

Moderato

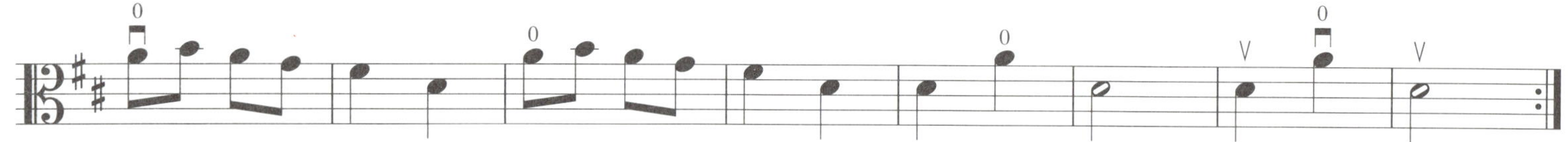

Chord, Harmony

Two or more pitches sounding at the same time form a **chord** or **harmony**. Throughout this book, **A** = Melody and **B** = Harmony.

89. BOIL 'EM CABBAGE DOWN – Orchestra Arrangement

American Fiddle Tune

Allegro

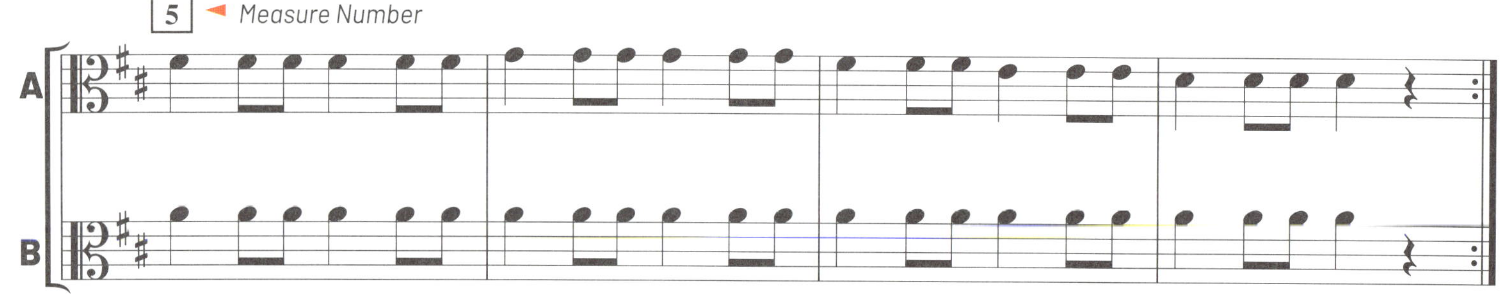

PERFORMANCE SPOTLIGHT

90. ENGLISH ROUND

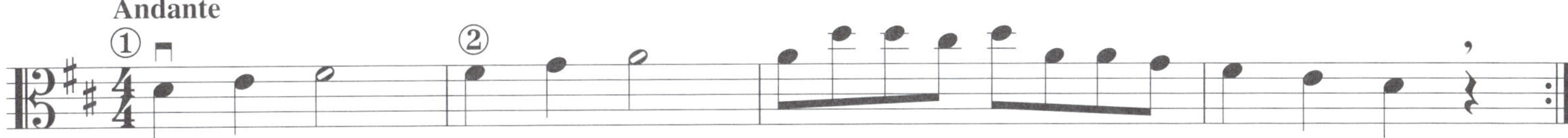

91. LIGHTLY ROW – Orchestra Arrangement

French composer **Jacques Offenbach** (1819–1880) was the originator of the **operetta** and played the cello. An **operetta** is a form of entertainment that combines several of the fine arts together: vocal and instrumental music, drama, dance, and visual arts. One of his most famous pieces is the "Can-Can" dance from *Orpheus And The Underworld*. This popular work was written in 1858, just three years before the start of the American Civil War (1861–1865).

HISTORY

92. CAN-CAN – Orchestra Arrangement

Jacques Offenbach
Arr. John Higgins

✔ What were the strong points of your performance?

G STRING NOTES

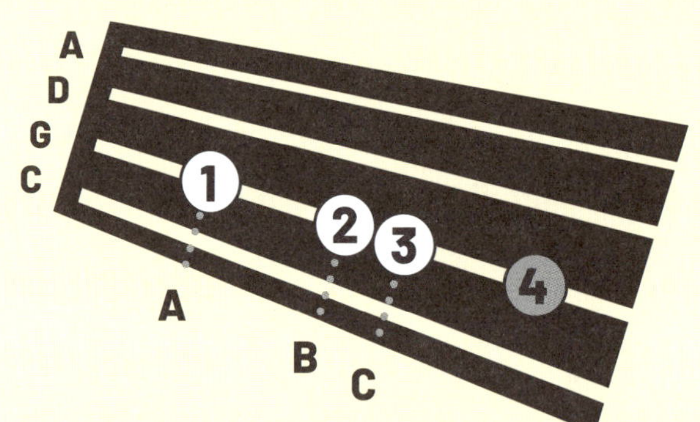

C is played with 3 fingers on the G string.

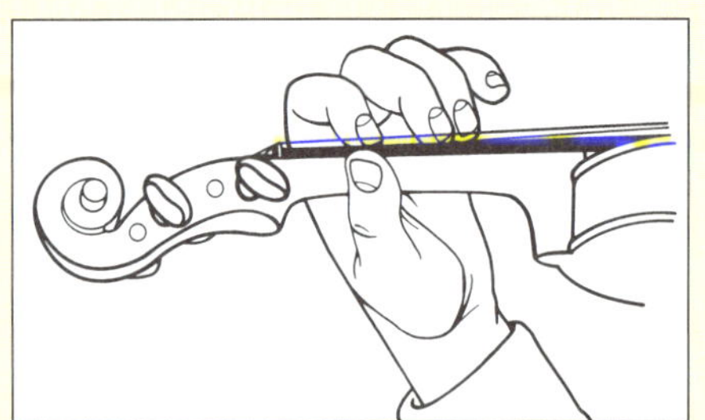

B is played with 2 fingers on the G string.

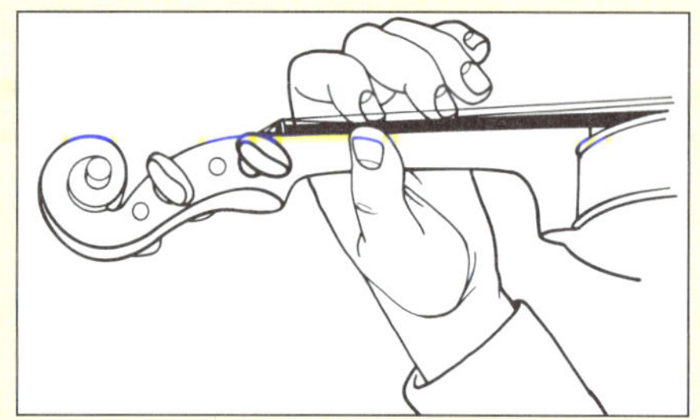

A is played with 1 finger on the G string.

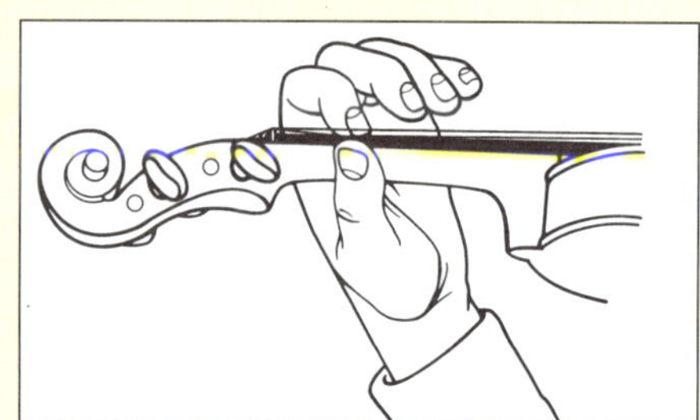

Listening Skills Play what your teacher plays. Listen carefully.

THEORY

Key Signature G MAJOR

Play all F's as F♯ (F-sharp) and all C's as C♮ (C-natural).

93. LET'S READ "G"

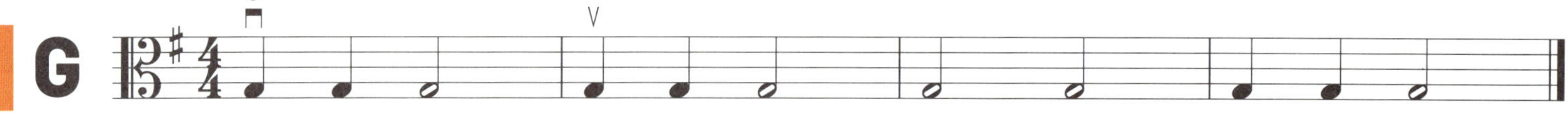

▲ *Play F♯'s and C♮'s in this key signature.*

94. LET'S READ "C" (C-natural)

95. LET'S READ "B"

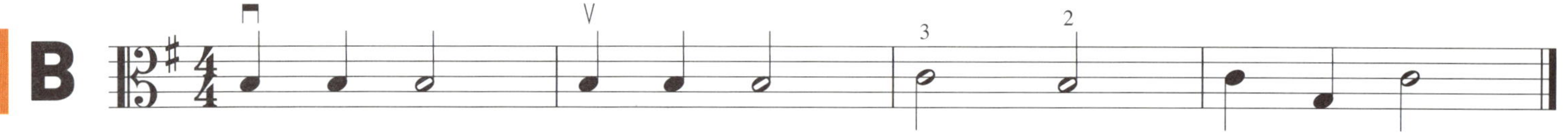

96. LET'S READ "A"

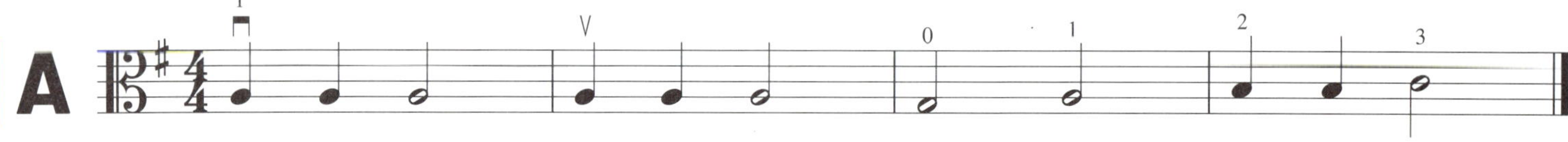

97. WALKING AROUND *Name the notes before you play.*

98. G MAJOR SCALE *Write the note names before you play.*

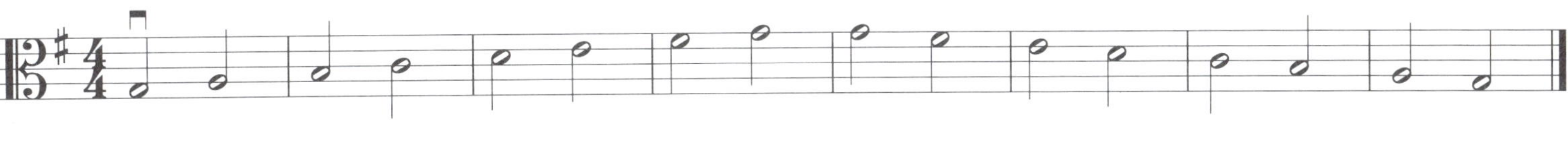

99. FOURTH FINGER D

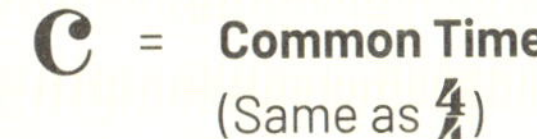

Conducting

Practice conducting this four-beat pattern.

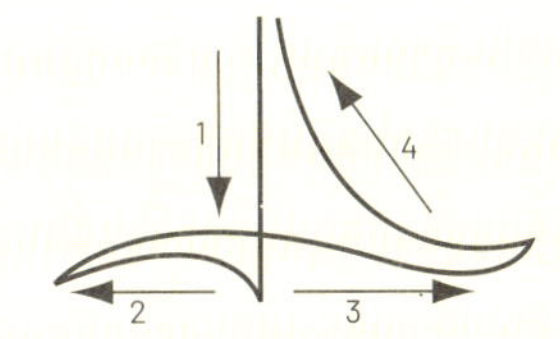

THEORY

100. LOW DOWN

101. BAA BAA BLACK SHEEP

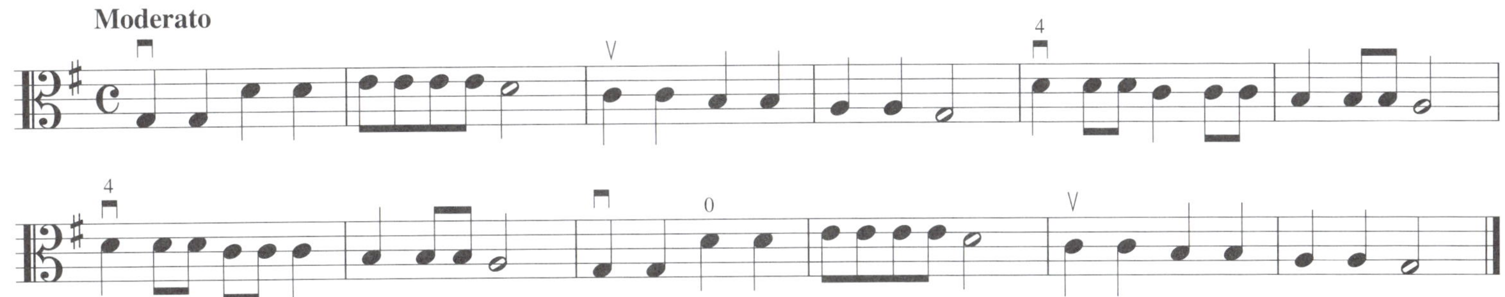

102. ESSENTIAL ELEMENTS QUIZ – THIS OLD MAN

American Folk Song

THEORY

Time Signature
(Meter)

3 = **3 beats** per measure
4 = ♩ or 𝄽 note gets one beat

Conducting

Practice conducting this three-beat pattern.

Dotted Half Note

𝅗𝅥. = 3 Beats of Sound
1 & 2 & 3 &

𝅗𝅥. ◄ **Dot**

A dot adds half the value of the note.

2 beats + 1 beat = 3 beats

103. RHYTHM RAP

Shadow bow and count before playing.

Count: 1 & 2 & 3 & 1 & 2 & 3 & 1 & 2 & 3 & 1 & 2 & 3 &

104. COUNTING THREES

Slow Bow *Slow Bow*

105. D MAJOR SCALE IN THREES

106. FRENCH FOLK SONG

French Folk Song

Moderato

107. ESSENTIAL ELEMENTS QUIZ – SAILOR'S SONG

English Sea Song

Allegro

▲ *Write in the correct time signature before you begin.*

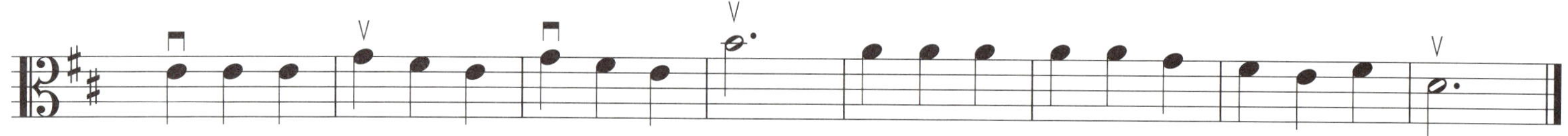

Tie

A **tie** is a curved line that connects notes of the **same** pitch. Play a single note for the combined counts of the tied notes.

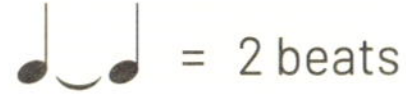

A **slur** is a curved line that connects two or more **different** pitches. Play slurred notes together in the same bow stroke.

110. SLURRING ALONG

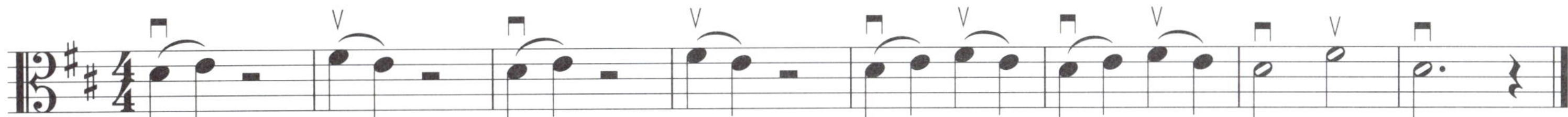

111. SMOOTH SAILING

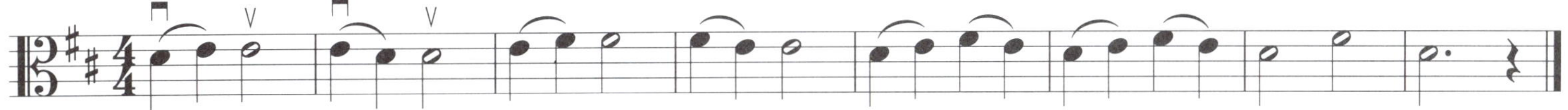

112. D MAJOR SLURS

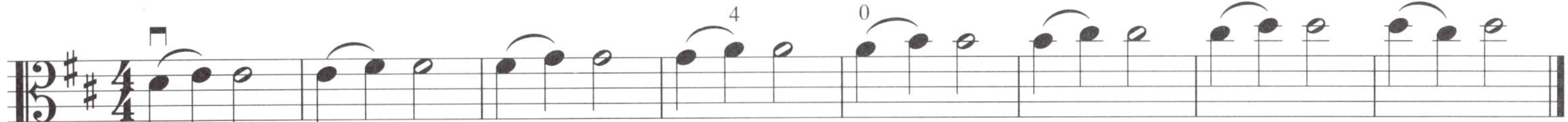

113. CROSSING STRINGS

114. GLIDING BOWS

115. UPSIDE DOWN

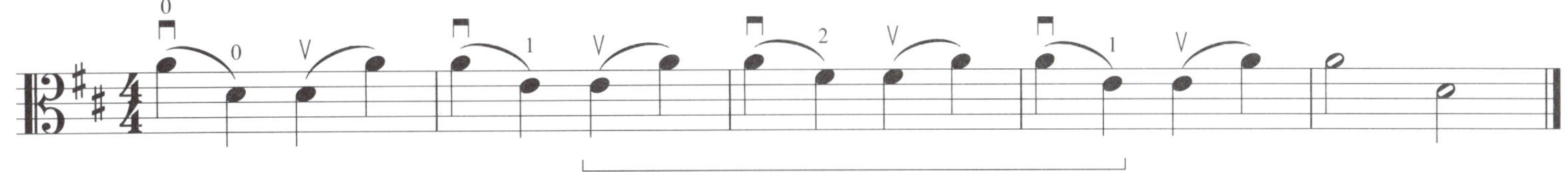

Upbeat

A note (or notes) that appears before the first full measure is called an **upbeat** (or **pickup**). The remaining beats are found in the last measure.

116. SONG FOR MARIA

HISTORY

Latin American music combines the folk music from South and Central America, the Caribbean Islands, African, Spanish, and Portuguese cultures. Melodies often feature a lively accompaniment by drums, maracas, and claves. Latin American styles have become part of jazz, classical, and rock music.

THEORY

D.C. al Fine

Play until you see the **D.C. al Fine**. Then go back to the beginning and play until you see **Fine** (*fee'- nay*). **D.C.** is the abbreviation for **Da Capo**, the Italian term for "return to the beginning." **Fine** is the Italian word for "the finish."

117. BANANA BOAT SONG

Caribbean Folk Song

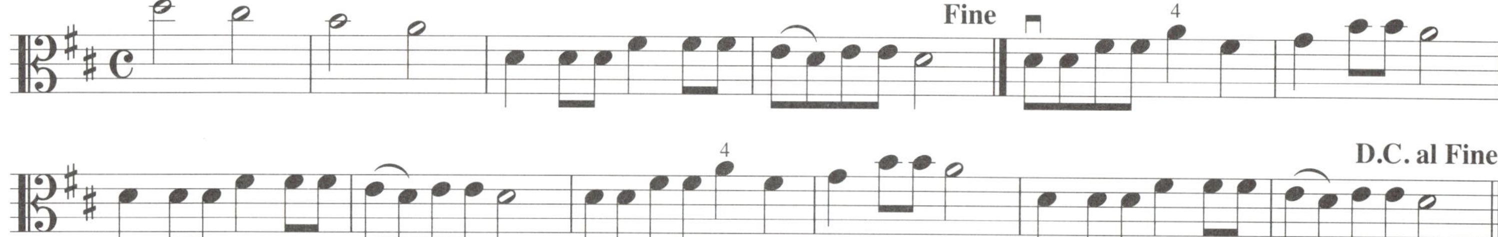

118. FIROLIRALERA – Orchestra Arrangement

Mexican Folk Song
Arr. John Higgins

SKILL BUILDERS – G Major

119.

120.

121.

122.

123.

▼ Slur three

124.

HISTORY

Far Eastern music comes from Malaysia, Indonesia, China and other areas. Historians believe the first orchestras, known as **gamelans**, existed in this region as early as the 1st century B.C. Today's gamelans include rebabs (spiked fiddles), gongs, xylophones, and a wide variety of percussion instruments.

125. JINGLI NONA

Far Eastern Folk Song

NEW FINGER PATTERN

Low 2nd Finger

Step 1
Shape your left hand as shown. Be certain your palm faces you. Notice your 2nd finger lightly touches your 1st finger.

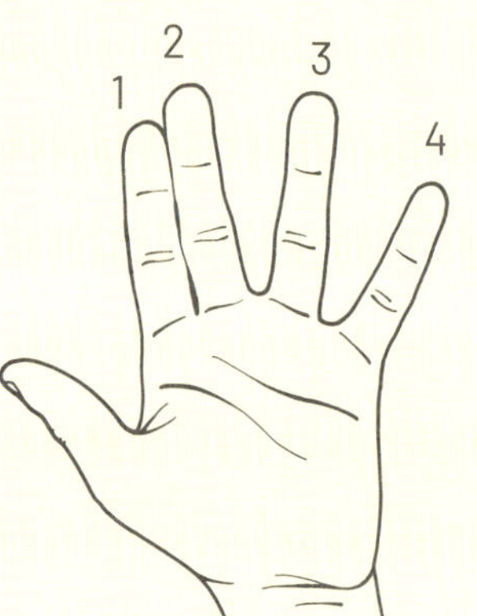

Step 2
Bring your hand to the fingerboard. Your 1st and 2nd fingers touch. There is a space between your 2nd and 3rd fingers, and between your 3rd and 4th fingers.

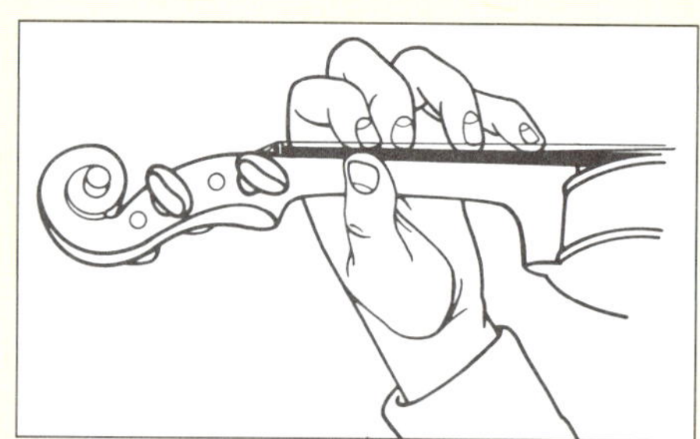

F
is played with low 2nd finger on the D string.

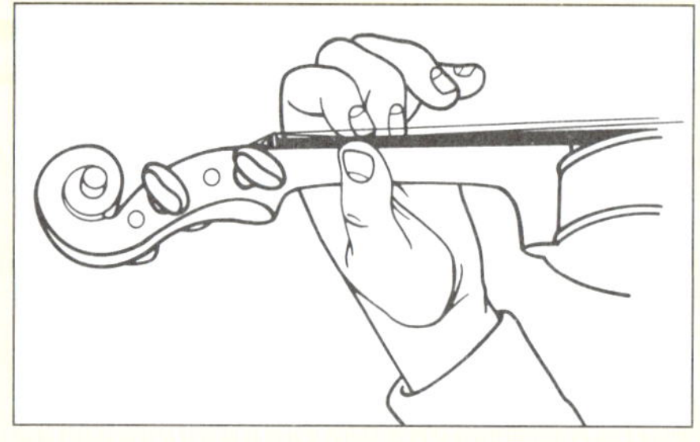

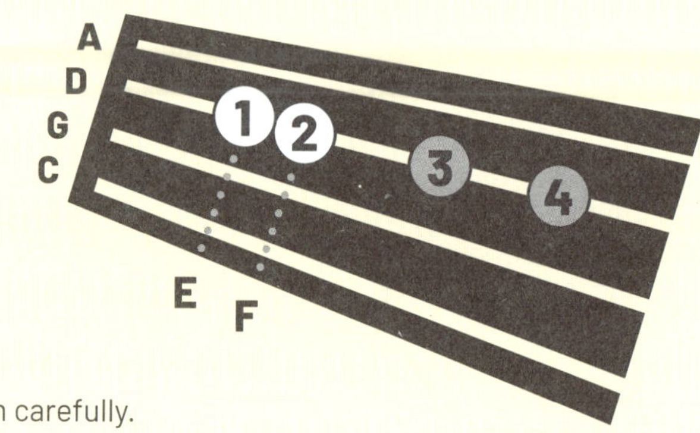

Listening Skills Play what your teacher plays. Listen carefully.

THEORY

Natural ♮
A **natural** sign cancels out a flat (♭) or a sharp (♯) and remains in effect for the entire measure.

126. LET'S READ "F" (F-natural)

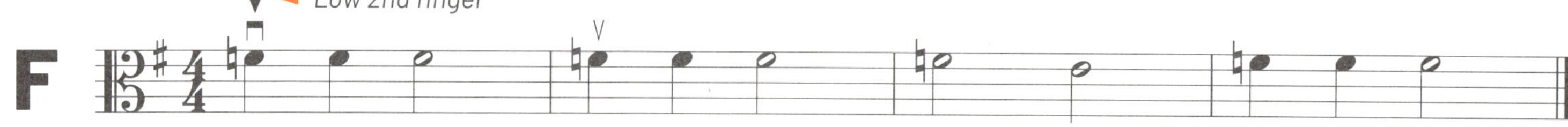

THEORY

Half Step A half step is the smallest distance between two notes.
Whole Step A whole step is two half steps combined.

127. HALF-STEPPIN' AND WHOLE-STEPPIN'

128. SPY GUY

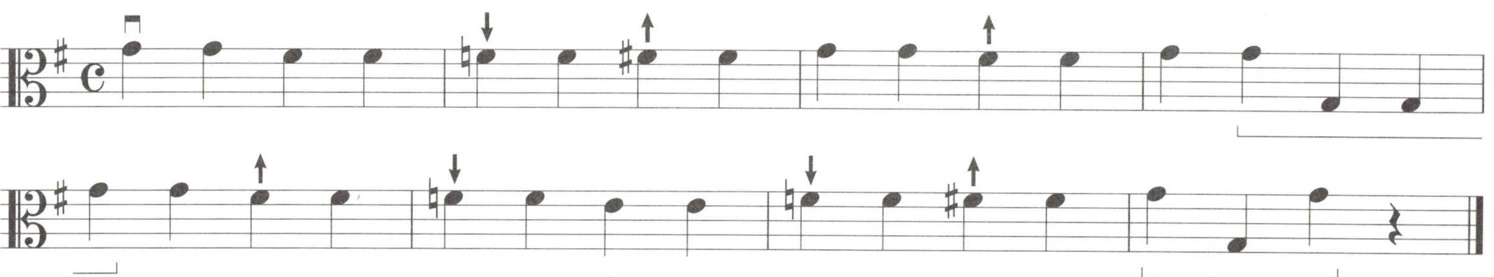

129. MINOR DETAILS

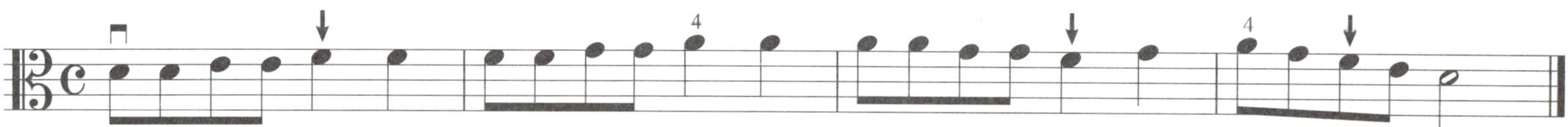

NEW FINGER PATTERN

Low 2nd Finger On The A String

Shape your left hand on the A string as shown.

C

is played with low 2nd finger on the A string.

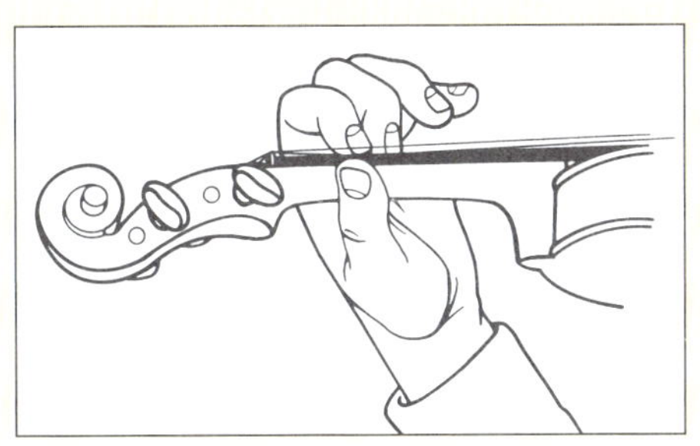

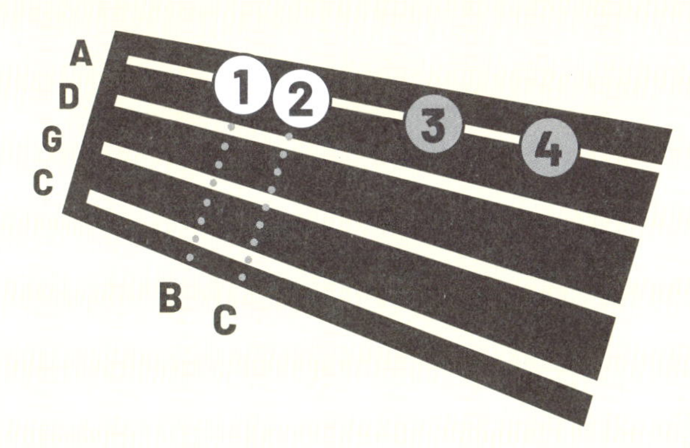

Listening Skills Play what your teacher plays. Listen carefully.

130. LET'S READ "C" (C-natural)

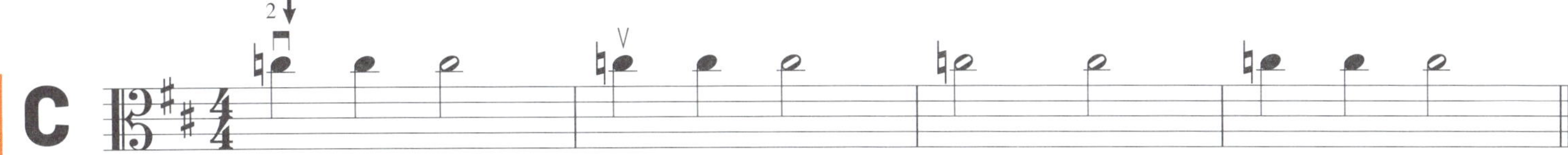

131. HALF STEP AND WHOLE STEP REVIEW

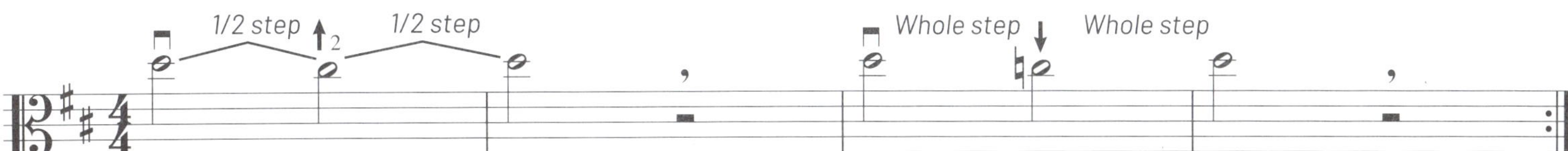

Chromatics **Chromatic notes** are altered with sharps, flats, and naturals.
A chromatic pattern is two or more notes in a sequence of half steps.

THEORY

132. CHROMATIC MOVES

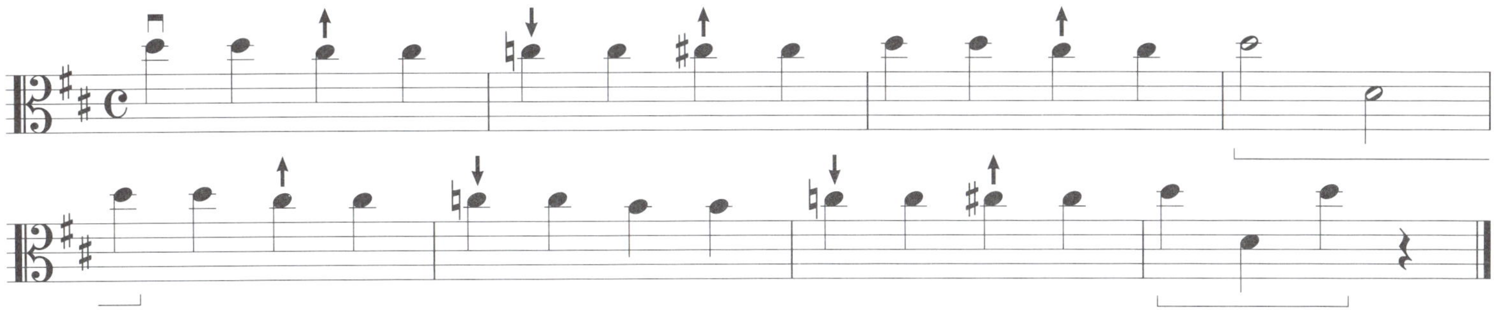

133. THE STETSON SPECIAL

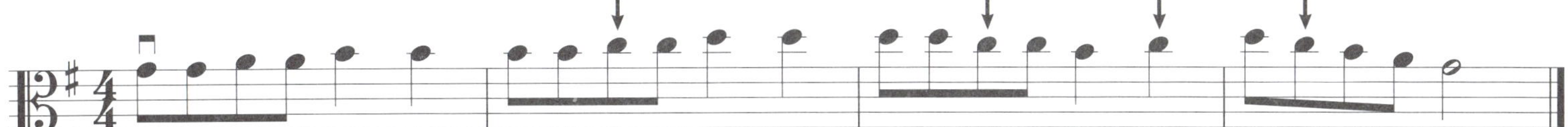

134. BLUEBIRD'S SONG

Texas Folk Song

Allegro

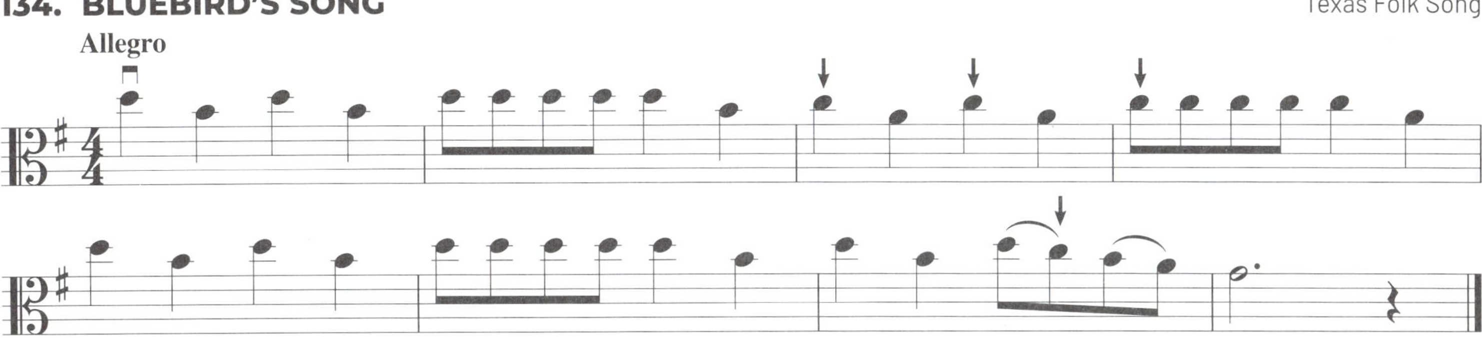

All notes are naturals.

135. C MAJOR SCALE – Round

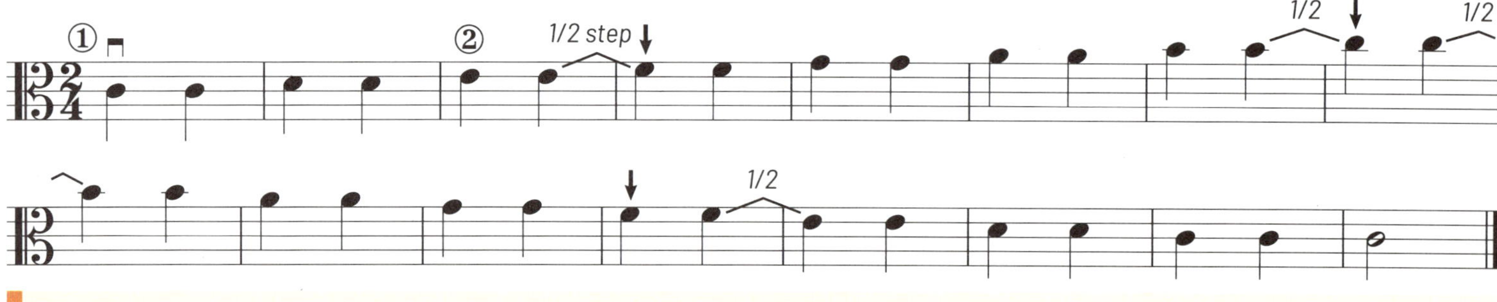

Duet A composition with two different parts, played together.

136. SPLIT DECISION – Duet

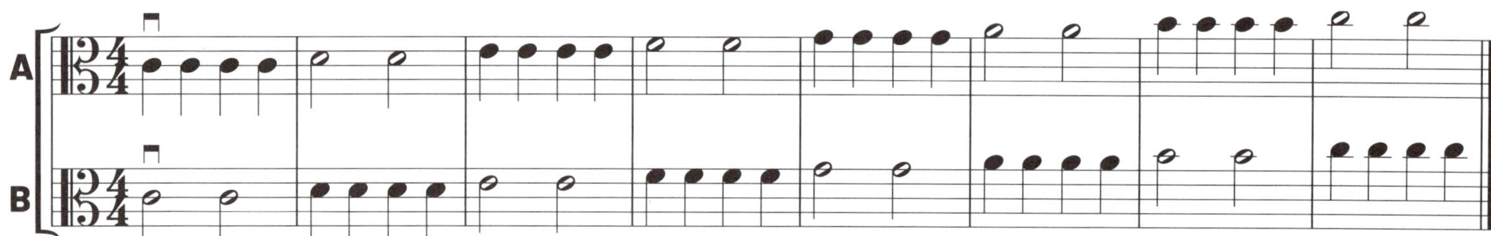

137. OAK HOLLOW

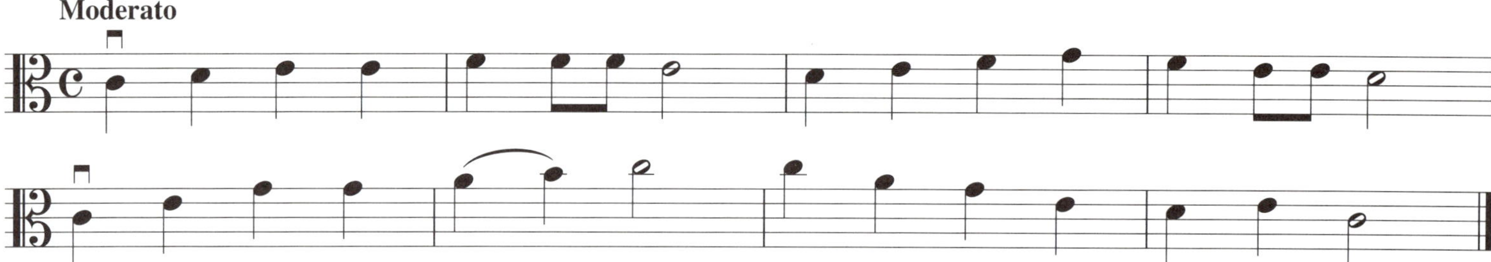

138. A-TISKET, A-TASKET

HISTORY

In the second half of the 1800s many composers tried to express the spirit of their own country by writing music with a distinct national flavor. Listen to the music of Russian composers such as Borodin, Tchaikovsky, and Rimsky-Korsakov. They often used folk songs and dance rhythms to convey their nationalism. Describe the sounds you hear.

139. ESSENTIAL ELEMENTS QUIZ – RUSSIAN FOLK TUNE

Russian Folk Song

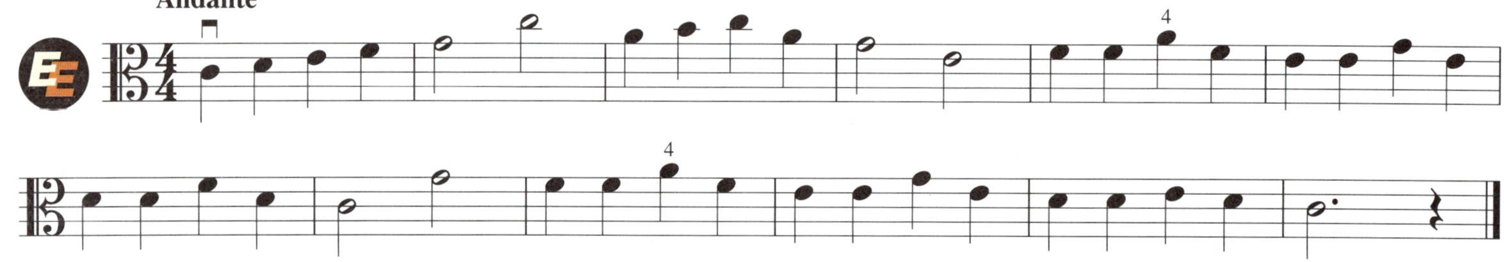

Alert This page mixes finger patterns. Watch for low 2nd finger (C♮) and high 2nd finger (F♯).

140. BINGO

18th Century English Game Song

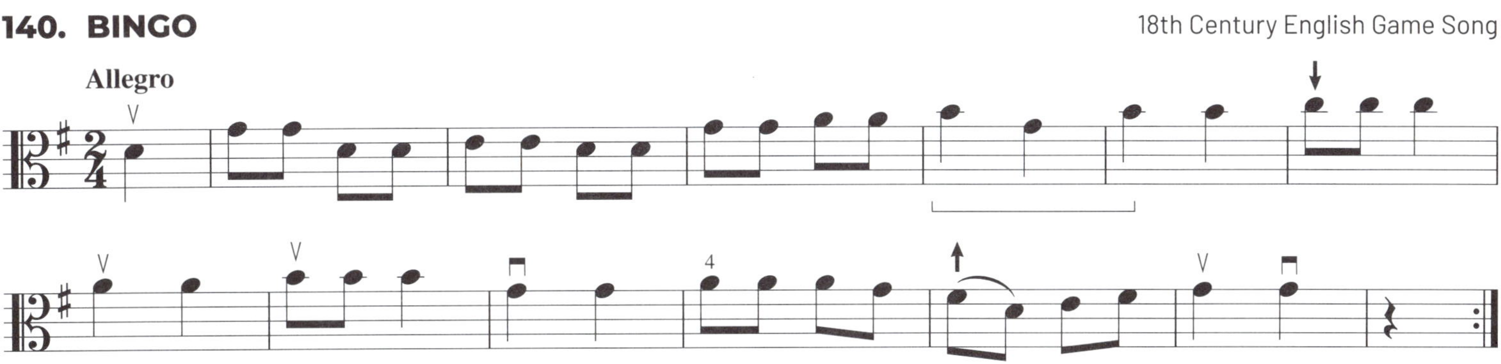

Where is beat 2?

HISTORY

English composer **Thomas Tallis** (1505-1585) served as royal court composer during the reigns of Henry VIII, Edward VI, Mary, and Elizabeth I. Composers and artists during this era wanted to recreate the artistic and scientific glories of ancient Greece and Rome. The great artist Michelangelo painted the Sistine Chapel during Tallis' lifetime. **Rounds** and **canons** were popular forms of music during the early 16th century. Divide into groups, and play or sing the *Tallis Canon* as a 4-part round.

141. TALLIS CANON – Round

Thomas Tallis

THEORY

Theme and Variations

Theme and Variations is a musical form where a theme, or melody, is followed by different versions of the same theme.

142. VARIATIONS ON A FAMILIAR SONG

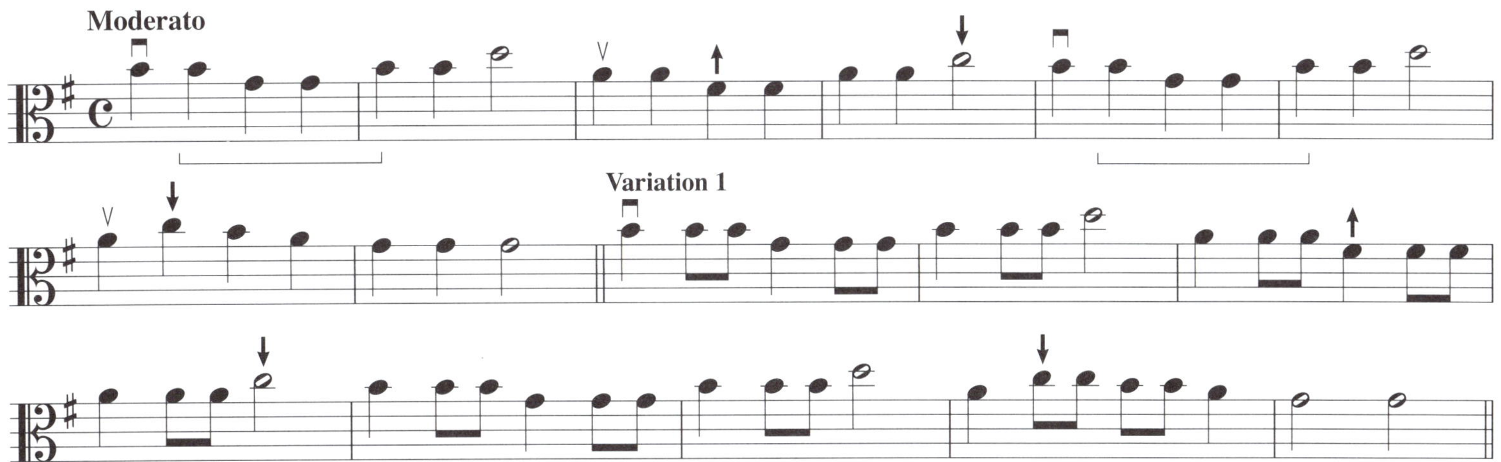

Variation 2 – *make up your own variation*

143. ESSENTIAL CREATIVITY – THE BIRTHDAY SONG

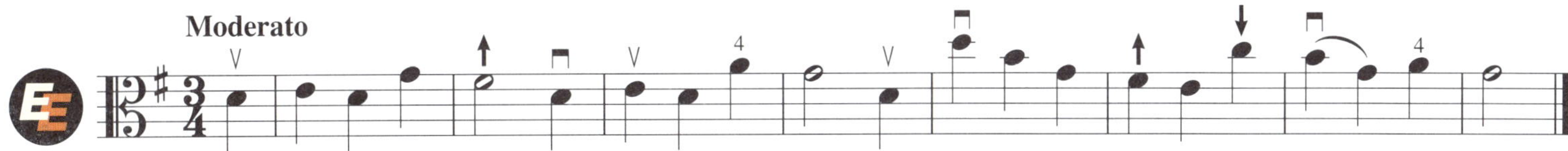

Now play the line again and create your own rhythm.

C STRING NOTES

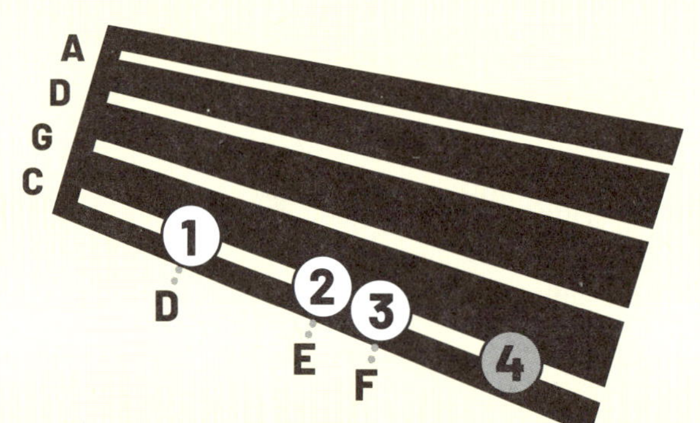

F is played with 3 fingers on the C string.

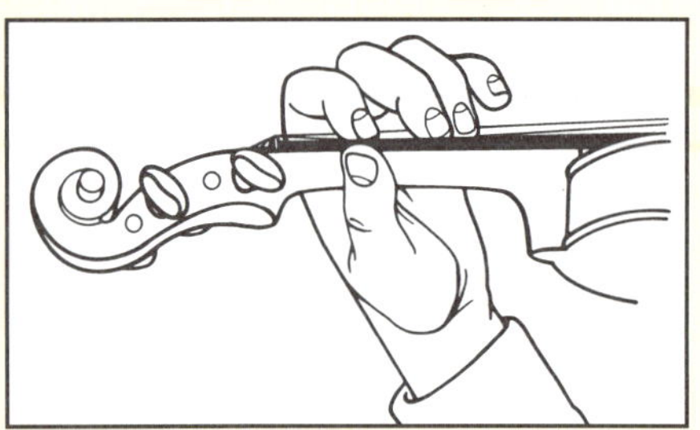

E is played with 2 fingers on the C string.

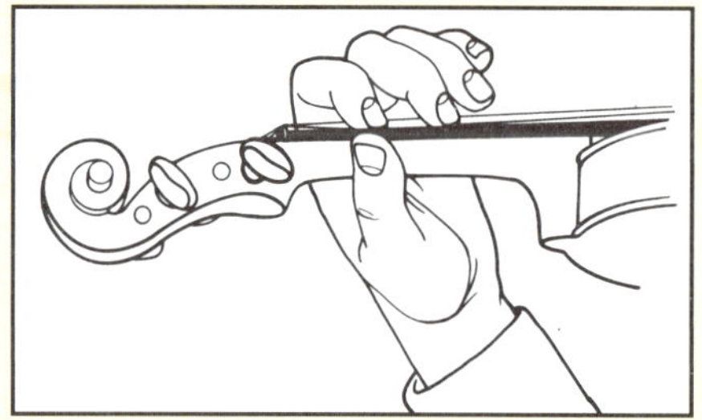

D is played with 1 finger on the C string.

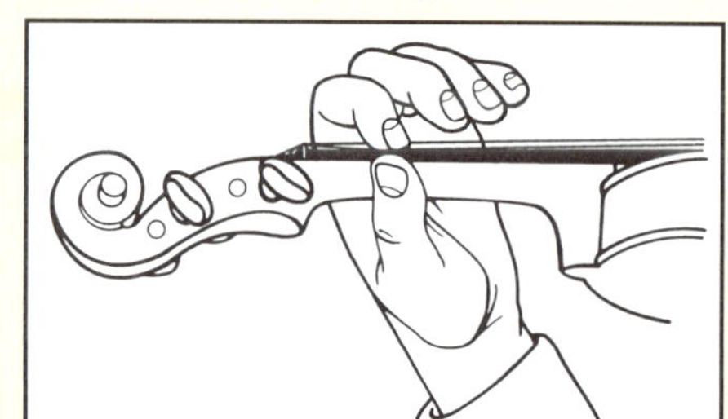

Listening Skills Play what your teacher plays. Listen carefully.

144. LET'S READ "C"

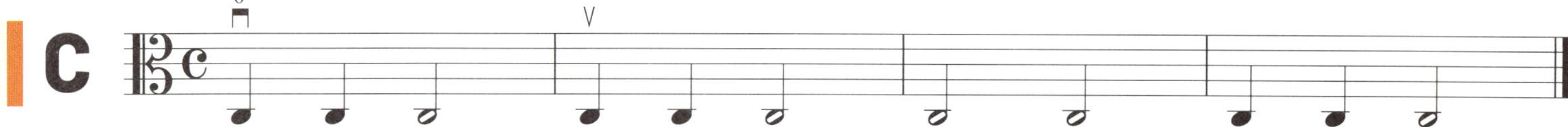

145. LET'S READ "F"

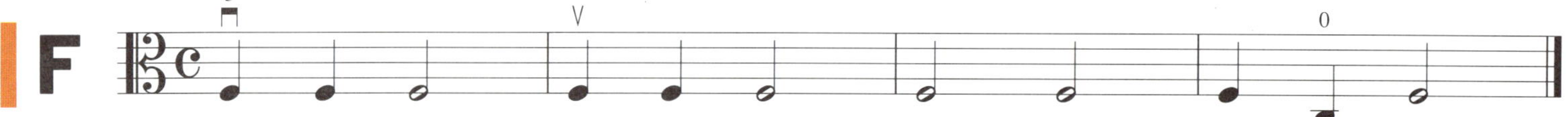

146. LET'S READ "E"

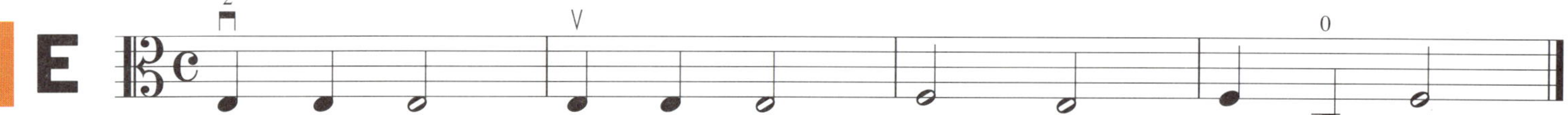

147. LET'S READ "D"

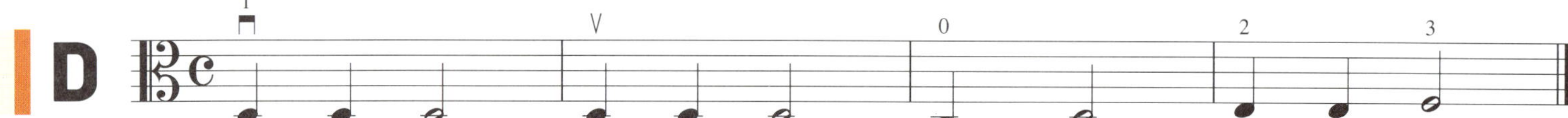

148. SIDE BY SIDE *Name the notes before you play.*

149. C MAJOR SCALE

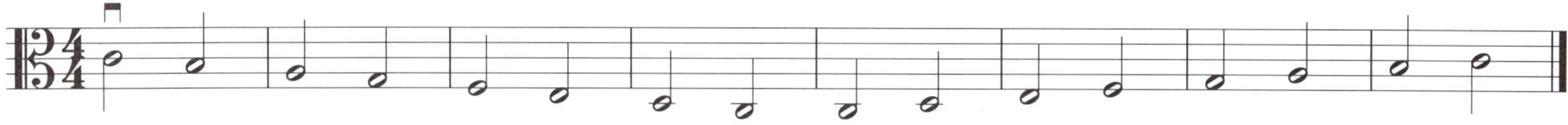

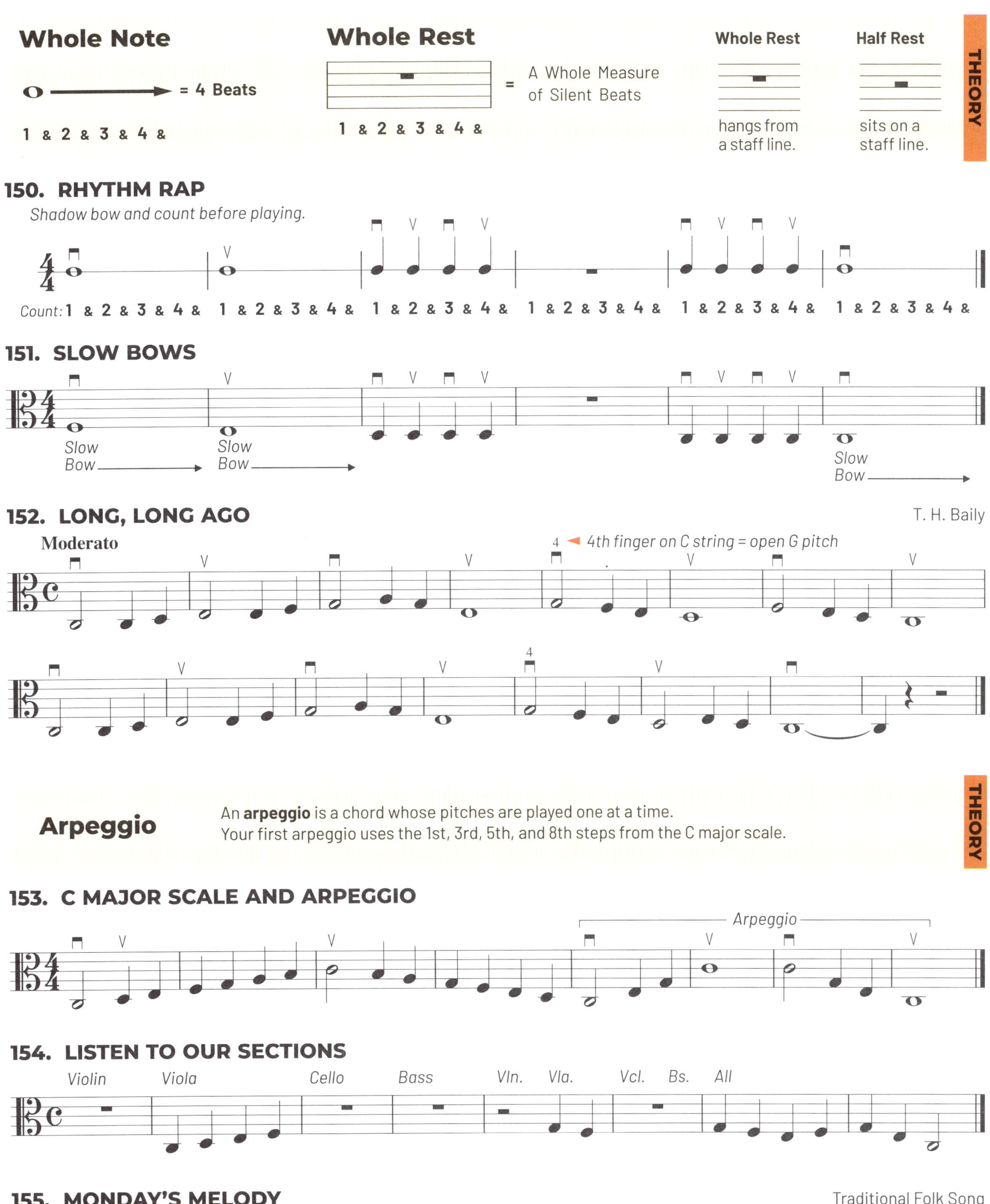

155. MONDAY'S MELODY

Traditional Folk Song

Moderato

4

0

Fine

D.C. al Fine

New Note

E

is played with 4 fingers on the A string.

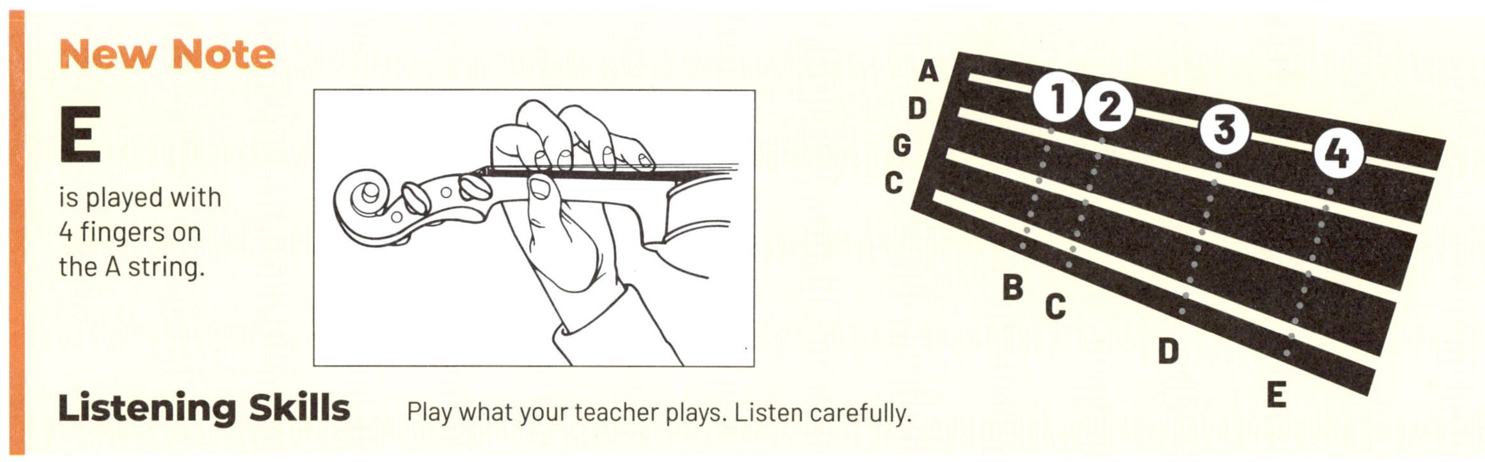

Listening Skills Play what your teacher plays. Listen carefully.

156. LET'S READ "E"

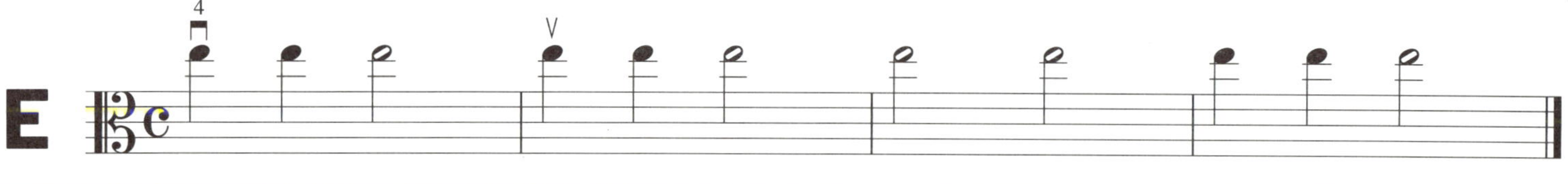

Special Viola Exercise

Write the note names below. Then, write stories using as many note names as possible. Share your work with orchestra friends.

Note Names:

Team Work Great musicians give encouragement to their fellow performers. Violin and bass players will now learn new challenging notes. The success of your orchestra depends on everyone's talent and patience. Play your best as these sections advance their musical technique.

157. LET'S READ "A" – Review

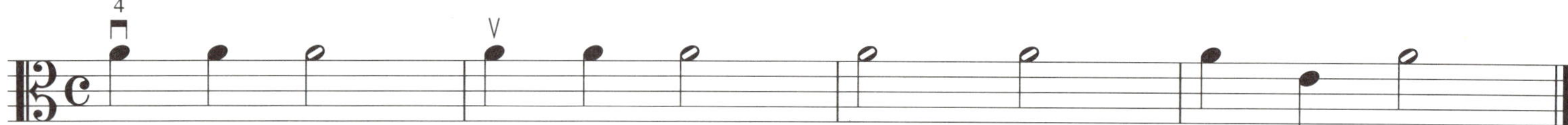

158. LET'S READ "G" – Review

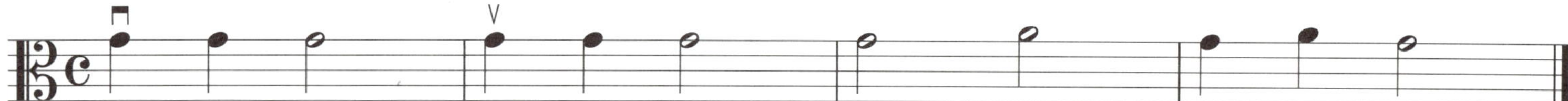

159. LET'S READ "F♯" (F-sharp) – Review

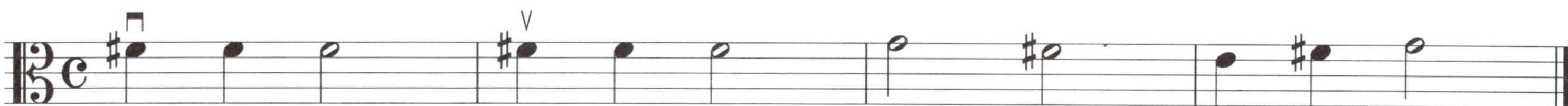

160. MOVING ALONG *Name the notes before you play.*

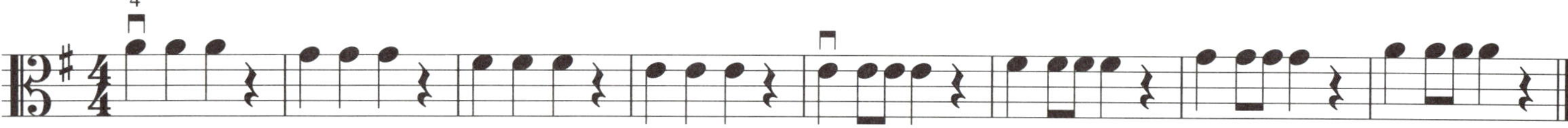

161. G MAJOR SCALE

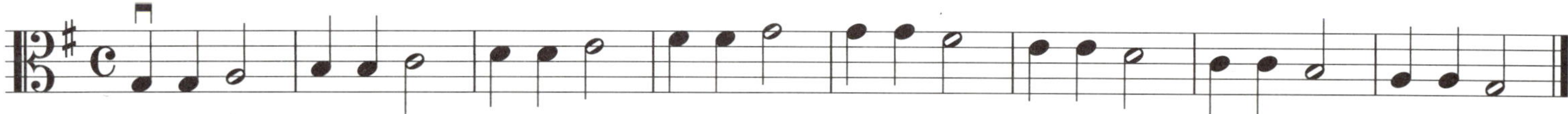

162. SHEPHERD'S HEY

English Folk Song

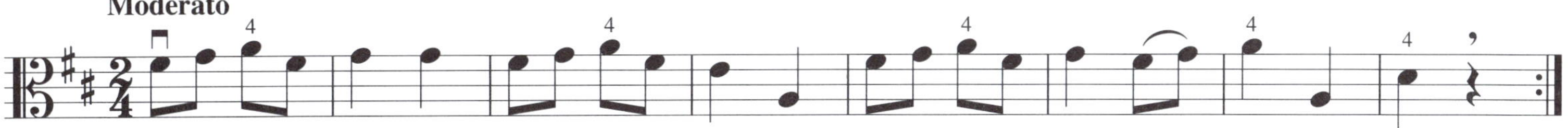

163. BIG ROCK CANDY MOUNTAIN

American Folk Song

Listening Skills

Play what your teacher plays. Listen carefully.

164. LET'S READ "B" – Review

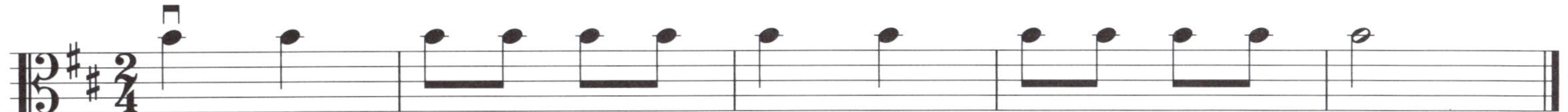

165. ICE SKATING

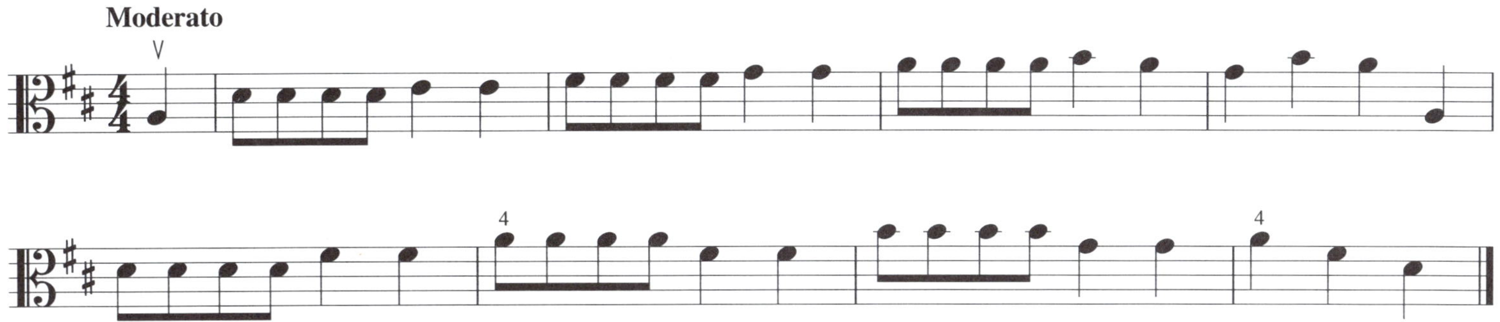

166. ESSENTIAL ELEMENTS QUIZ – ACADEMIC FESTIVAL OVERTURE THEME

Johannes Brahms

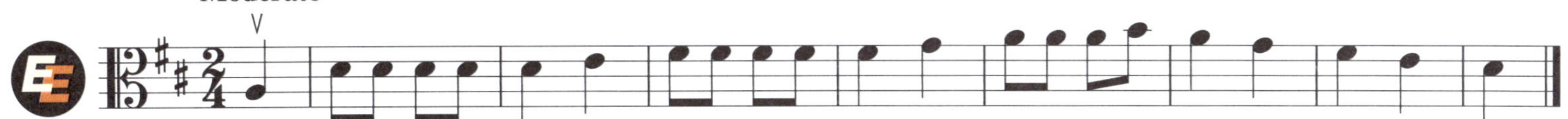

Additional bonus songs are available online. See the inside front cover for details.

Staccato

Staccato notes are marked with a dot above or below the note. A staccato note is played with a stopped bow stroke. Listen for a space between staccato notes.

167. PLAY STACCATO

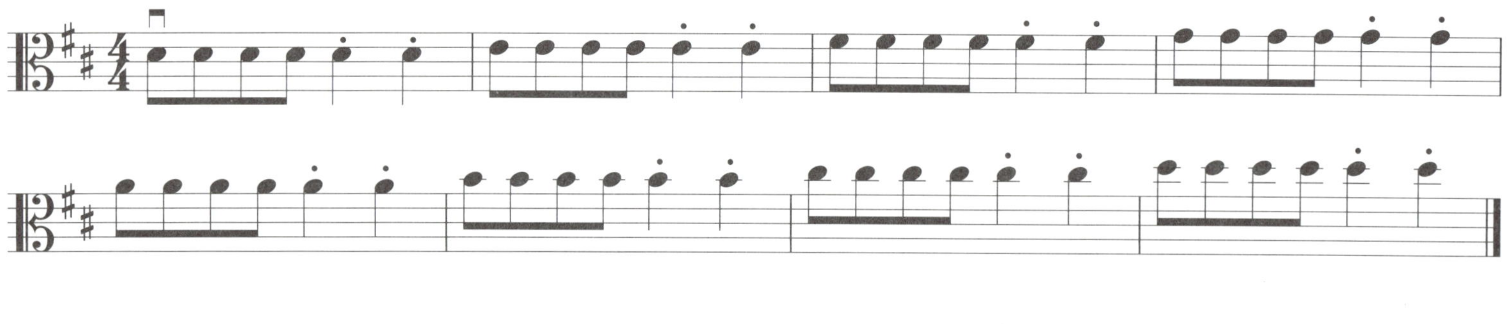

168. ARKANSAS TRAVELER

Southern American Folk Song

Allegro

SKILL BUILDERS – G Major

169.

170.

171.

172.

173.

Hooked Bowing

Hooked bowing is two or more notes played in the same direction with a stop between each note.

174. HOOKED ON D MAJOR

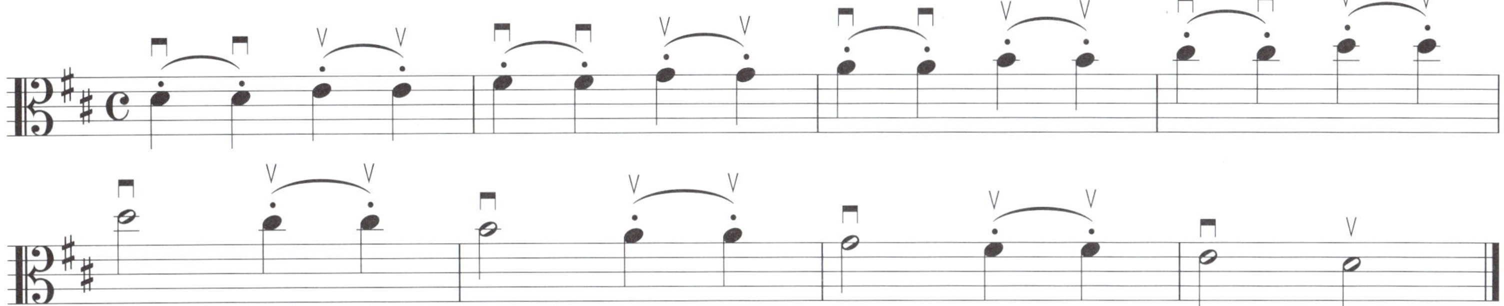

175. WALTZING BOWS

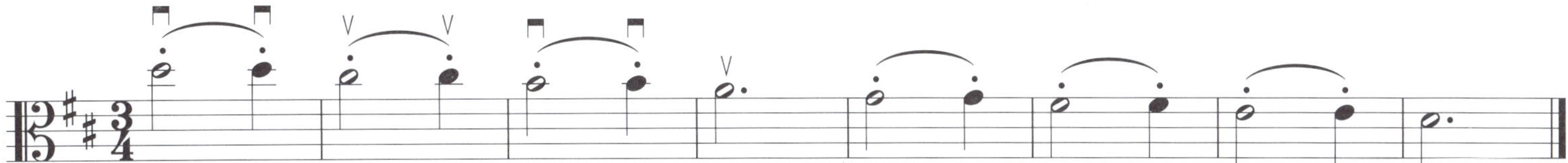

176. POP GOES THE WEASEL

American Folk Song

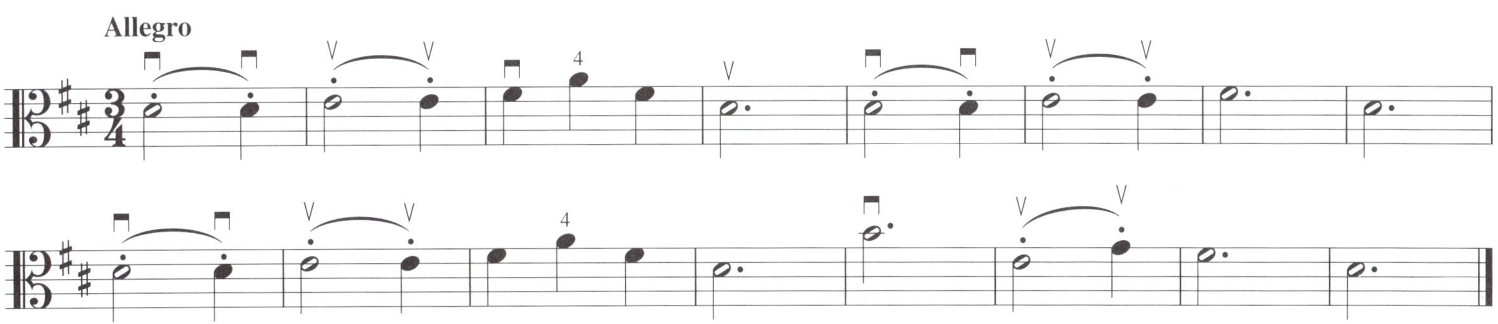

SKILL BUILDERS – C Major

Dynamics

Dynamics tell us what volume to play or sing.

f (*forte*) Play loudly. Add more weight to the bow.

p (*piano*) Play softly. Remove weight from the bow.

181. FORTE AND PIANO

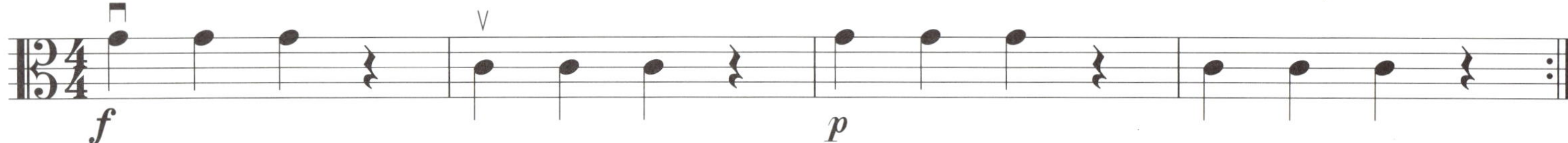

182. SURPRISE SYMPHONY THEME

Franz Josef Haydn

SKILL BUILDERS – Scales and Arpeggios

Add your own dynamics to any of the lines below.

183. D MAJOR

184. G MAJOR

185. G MAJOR (*Upper Octave – violin*)

186. C MAJOR

187. C MAJOR

PERFORMANCE SPOTLIGHT

188. CRIPPLE CREEK – Orchestra Arrangement (A = Melody and B = Harmony)

American Folk Song
Arr. Michael Allen

Africa is a large continent made up of many nations, and African folk music is as diverse as its many cultures. This folk song is from Kenya. The words describe warriors as they prepare for battle. Listen to examples of African folk music and describe the sound.

HISTORY

189. TEKELE LOMERIA – Orchestra Arrangement

Kenyan Warrior Song
Arr. John Higgins

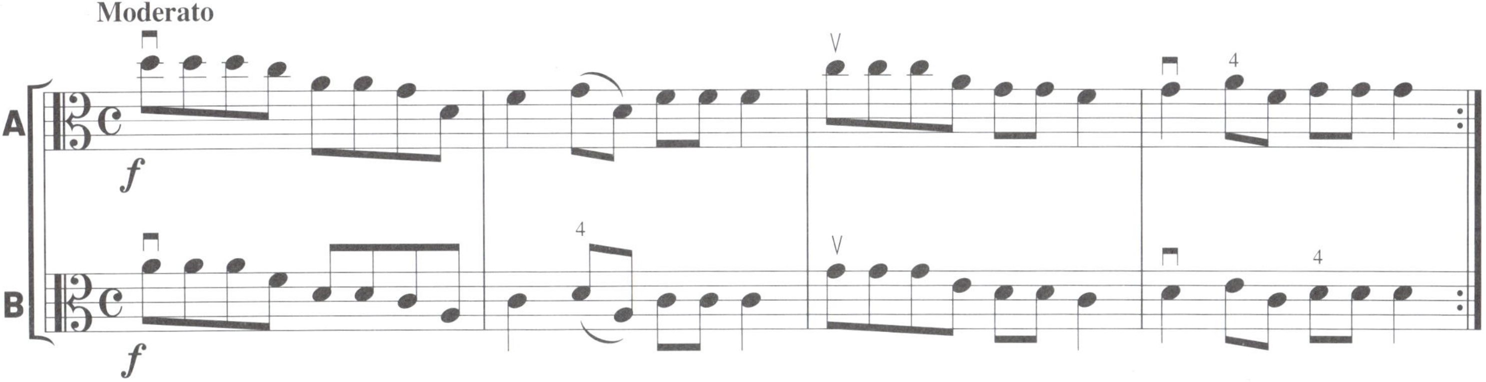

PERFORMANCE SPOTLIGHT

HISTORY

Italian composer **Gioachino Rossini** (1792–1868) wrote some of the world's favorite operas. "William Tell" was Rossini's last opera, and its popular theme is still heard on television.

190. WILLIAM TELL OVERTURE – Orchestra Arrangement

Gioachino Rossini
Arr. John Higgins

Allegro

A
B

Fine

9

D.C. al Fine

191. ROCKIN' STRINGS – Orchestra Arrangement

John Higgins

PERFORMANCE SPOTLIGHT

192. SIMPLE GIFTS – Orchestra Arrangement

Shaker Folk Song
Arr. John Higgins

PERFORMANCE SPOTLIGHT

Solo with Piano Accompaniment

A solo is a composition written for one player, often with piano accompaniment. This solo was written by **Johann Sebastian Bach** (1685-1750). You and a piano accompanist can perform for the orchestra, your school, your family and other occasions. When you have learned the piece well, try memorizing it. Performing for an audience is an excellent part of being involved in music.

193. MINUET IN C – Solo

Johann Sebastian Bach
Arr. by John Higgins

Improvisation

Improvisation is the art of freely creating your own music as you play.

194. RHYTHM JAM *Using the following notes, improvise your own rhythms.*

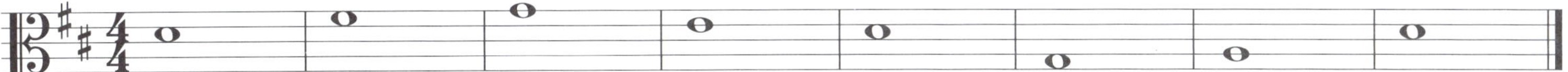

195. INSTANT MELODY *Using the following notes, improvise your own melody (Line A), to go with the accompaniment (Line B).*

VIOLA FINGERING CHART

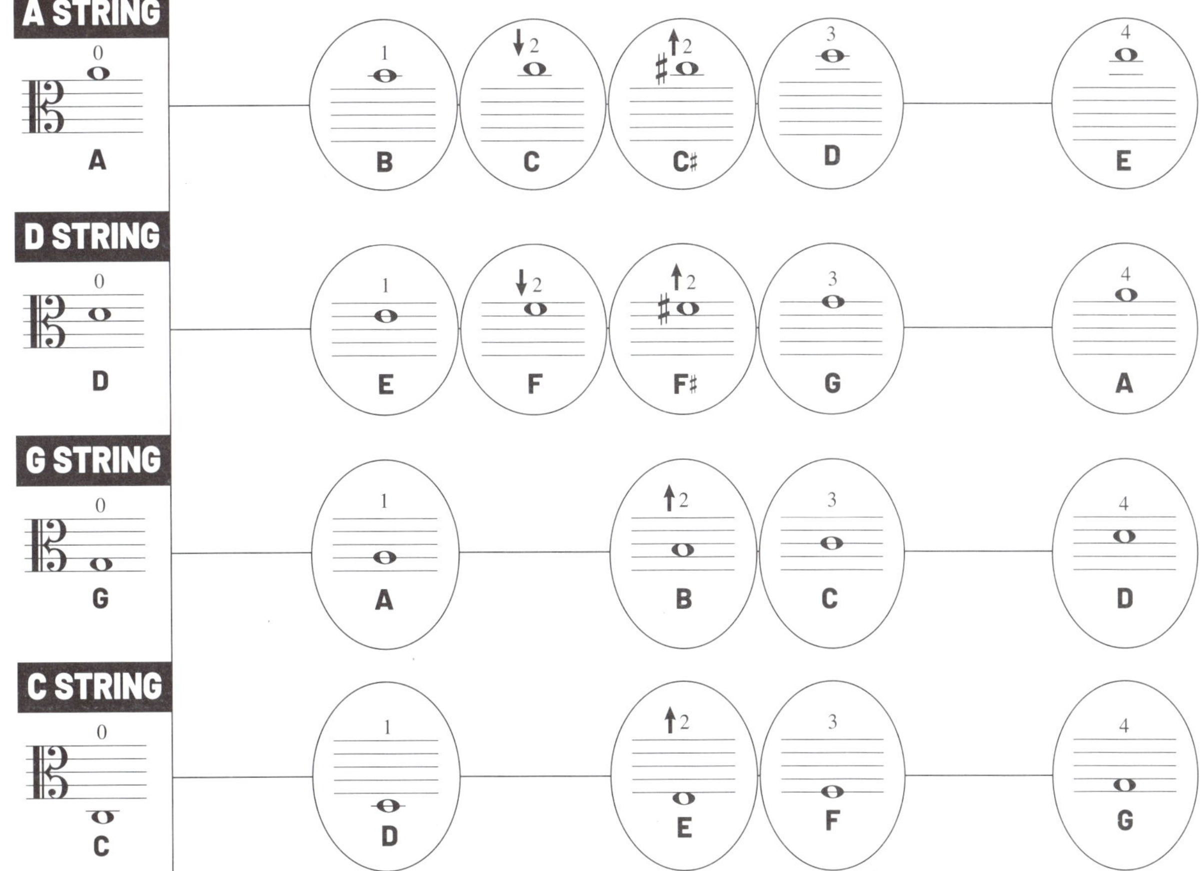

Reference Index

Definitions (pg.)

Composers

World Music